American Poets in Profile

The Giver of Morning, on Dave Smith
Dissolve to Island, on John Logan

Layle Silbert

Dissolve To Island:
on the Poetry of John Logan

Edited by Michael Waters

Ford-Brown & Co., Publishers
Houston, Texas: 1984

Printed in the United States of America

American Poets Profile Series Number 2

First Printing, November 1984

Library of Congress Cataloguing in Publication Data

Waters, Michael, 1949-
    Dissolve to Island: On the Poetry of John Logan

The American Poets Profile Series

Library of Congress Catalogue Card Number: 83-050545
ISBN: 0-918644-35-6 Paper
ISBN: 0-918644-36-4 Cloth

The publication of this book is supported by a grant from the National Endowment for the Arts in Washington, D.C., a Federal Agency.

Acknowledgments

Grateful acknowledgment is made to the following presses and magazines for permission to reprint material:

Poems from *Only the Dreamer Can Change the Dream: Selected Poems* are reprinted with permission of The Ecco Press. Copyright © 1981 by John Logan.

Poems from *The Bridge of Change: Poems 1974-1980* are reprinted with permission of BOA Editions, Ltd. Copyright © 1981 by John Logan.

New poems by John Logan are reprinted with permission of the author. "The Transformation" appeared in *The New Republic*. "The Piano Scholar" appeared in *The Massachusetts Review*. "Avocado" appeared in *The Seattle Review*. "A Month of Saints" appeared in *The Kenyon Review*. "Staying Awake" appeared in *The Brockport Review*. "Manhattan Movements" appeared in *Memphis State Review*.

Much of the material in Marvin Bell's "Starting in Chicago" appeared previously in "My Twenties in Chicago: A Memoir," published by *Triquarterly* (Spring/Summer 1984), © 1984 by Marvin Bell. "Starting in Chicago" copyright © 1984 by Marvin Bell.

The excerpt on the back cover is reprinted with the kind permission of Farrar Straus Giroux from *Babel to Byzantium* by James Dickey. Copyright © 1968 by James Dickey.

The covers of each of the books are reprinted with permission of the publishers as noted:

Only the Dreamer Can Change the Dream: Selected Poems with permission of The Ecco Press. Cover after an original photograph by Aaron Siskind.

The Bridge of Change: Poems 1974-1980 with permission of BOA Editions, Ltd. Cover after an original photograph by Joseph Jachna, Door County, Wisconsin, 1970.

Manhattan Movements cover designed by Steven Ford Brown.

Contents

Dissolve to Island: An Introduction

I can be very specific. On Wednesday evening, October 23, 1969, Galway Kinnell read his poems in the Gold Room of the Communications Building at the State University of New York at Brockport. I was nineteen and mesmerized. The reading was generous-spirited, intelligent, and lit with a language that resonated throughout the auditorium. I was beginning to write my own poems then, and listened with an intensity that bordered on religious fervor. I believed that if I listened hard enough, some secret of skillful language-manipulation would be revealed to me, and I would be initiated into the subtle brotherhood of poets. I was a very foolish young man.

Midway through the reading, Kinnell looked into the audience and paused. "I see my friend John Logan," he said. Then: "John, will you read us a poem?" And a few rows away from where I sat, an embarrassed, awkward, somewhat ungainly man stood up—I think of this first glimpse of John Logan now whenever I read his lovely "Moor Swan"— and began reciting, from memory, in a voice that trembled each syllable, "Three Moves":

> Three moves in six months and I remain
> the same.
> Two homes made two friends.
> The third leaves me with myself again.
> (We hardly speak.)

I was stunned. I could feel each syllable on the skin of my arms, on my face. Each word breathed its own texture as Logan wove his poem, swaying slightly where he stood, reading as much for himself as for the audience, for Kinnell. And for the first time I understood . . . *what*?

It would be years, after I'd managed to make a few true poems of my own, before I could begin to articulate what had been given to me that evening.

It wasn't until the following April that I was able to hear John Logan give a full reading of his poems. I had arranged, through a student organization, to bring John back to Brockport. By then I was familiar with his work—I'd bought *Ghosts of the Heart* (I asked Logan during his visit to sign the book. The inscription reads: "for Michael with thanks for an evening of reading impossible without him— 20 April '70 John Logan") and *The Zigzag Walk* (that inscription reads: "for Michael with hopes for his own works" [!]) and read them again and again. Several poems had been committed, without my realizing it, to memory. Their music was that insistent.

Hearing Logan's voice—at his reading and on the page—changed the way I'd hear poems in the future, changed the way I'd read them aloud or to myself, changed the way, finally, I'd make my own poems. If this sounds a bit foolish, forgive me, but Logan's poems were the first to rise a bit off the page for me. I could taste each word as I pronounced it, feel its shape like a marble or bit of gravel on my tongue. For the first time, the possibilities inherent in language presented themselves to me. For the first time, although I'd fooled myself before, I fell in love with words. For this gift I will remain forever grateful.

I know this might have happened sooner or later, if not through Logan then through Kinnell, or Wilbur, or Snodgrass, or Creeley, all poets I read and heard read that same year. But the fact remains that it was John's poems that spoke to me clearly, precisely, intimately, that filled me with music, that bridged the distance between the page and the reader.

If the work comes first, as it must, and if the writer must labor in solitude, must "dissolve to island"—the phrase appears in "The Bridge of Change"—in order to create, then the work becomes a bridge to other islands, a means of communion and brotherhood among writers, among us all. John Logan was the first writer to express such yearning to me, and to make me see that an artist could express such yearning without sentimentality, without apology. The language *was* reliable, ever burgeoning, and would not betray the writer who placed his faith in it.

John Logan's poems continue to be remarkable gifts in my life, and this book—from someone less young and, with luck, less foolish—means to offer thanks, to share such gifts with you.

Michael Waters
Salisbury, Maryland

Dissolve To Island

John Logan, South Bend, Indiana, 1952.

Starting in Chicago

MARVIN BELL

In 1960 I registered for a poetry writing course taught by John Logan one night a week in the downtown center of The University of Chicago. He was living at home in those days, with a wife and nine children and a dog, in South Bend, Indiana, where he taught for Notre Dame. He had learned to do school work aboard the bus while he commuted the ninety-five miles of toll road between South Bend and Chicago.

I confess that I knew nothing about John Logan. In our first class, he rattled off a list of his publications. But if he was nervous about getting the respect he deserved, we were as anxious to receive the atten-

13

tion we didn't deserve but had paid for. I myself had signed up for the course in part to satisfy the requirement that I be a registered student during the quarter of my M.A. examination.

Dorothy and I were living together. We had a fair-haired infant from my brief first marriage, and we were both in John's class. We ate spaghetti with him, and soon we were being treated as the official young newlyweds of the group. One evening after class, meeting up in a bar with John and his very close, longtime friends, Bob and Dorothy Jungels, then also from South Bend, John turned to me suddenly and asked the date of our anniversary.

How could I tell him that we weren't married? It was 1960. John was thin, hardly drank, rarely swore, displayed a scholarly sensibility at times, and didn't have a driver's license. I had been around the block and, to tell the truth, my young, naive self thought John a bit square. So I gave him a made-up date: July 9. John was astonished. "That's MY anniversary," he said, and, yes, it was also the Jungels'. We ordered beers to celebrate our mutual anniversaries. Later, when Dorothy and I married, we made certain to do it on July 9.

Years passed before I confessed to John. He pretended, I think, to be shocked. We were driving downhill to a party in San Francisco when I told him. By then, much had changed. For example, he had learned to drive, sort of.

A great driver, no. But he was the best reader of poetry in the country then, back when he taught in Chicago. When he read aloud our poor poems, they sounded beautiful and serious, and he took seriously our adolescent psyches and verbal gamesmanship. We felt the poetic possibilities in the air, and we loved this needful man who treated our words with such gentleness.

Near the end of the quarter, we decided to write poems about a single subject. I suggested the circus, which was in town—a lousy idea. Nevertheless, we handed over our poems a week later. John brooded over the assignment and finally wrote "The Thirty-Three Ring Circus," a series of formal epiphanies and a graphic view of the underside of a circus.

Then the course was over. John invited me to join the Poetry Seminar, a group of Chicago poets who met once a month in the offices of Jordan Miller's Midwest Clipping Association. Dennis Schmitz was part of it, and Bill Knott. Charles Simic passed through. Jessie Kachmar usually wore a large hat, and she read to us a poem in which a spider in her bathtub wrote in "spider gothic." Naomi Lazard and Irene Keller were there, as were Roger Aplon, William Hunt, Barbara Harr, James Bonk, Peter L. Simpson, Stuart McCarrell and others. We had our official Political Poet. Sometimes, Jessie would turn my free-verse poems on their sides and say that they resembled the skyline of Chicago. Probably did. We passed around carbon copies of our poems and stayed each session as long as it took to discuss at least one poem by each person. Most people thought Jim Murphy (who was to die in a car crash) to be the best of us.

John was still a practicing Catholic. He was writing the poems which would go into *Spring of the Thief*. On his birthday, I gave him a "first class" relic, supposed to be a piece of bone from Saint Augustine, procured through Dorothy's grandmother, who had Church connections. I suppose it was a silly gift, finally. I can recreate the conversation around the moment when I gave it to him, but I still don't know how he felt about such a thing.

Since then, I have seen John in many places. He has survived as he has had to. He wrote "Susannah" (later changed to "Suzanne") in a little house which was part tower and in which my family and I were then living in Iowa City. I know that it is "Susannah" that he wrote there. Yet I have often thought that "Three Moves" came into being there also. Maybe because he read it in our home when the poem was new. Maybe because I published it in *The North American Review*. Perhaps because I once read it into a microphone at WSUI, the University radio station, while an engineer stood ready to pull the plug if he heard any bad words like those he had heard me say the previous week in reading the poems of Allen Ginsberg. I decided to tell the audience of my problem, then read the poem with "suitable" changes:

> Poor s.'s-o.-b.ing ducks.
> You're all hyperboleed up.

(I like to think that each listener heard the correct words. Later, the engineer moved to Utah.)

Originally, the title "Three Moves" led straight into the poem and was not repeated in the first line. Also, John muted a rhyme for the sake of sense when, in line thirty-four, he substituted "climb" for "dive."

"Three Moves" is about doing without the Catholic Church, yet without abandoning some of its fundamental ideas. It utters the almost unspeakably lonely self-reflection of its author during that time. It defines God in terms of friendship, and it defines friendship in terms of forgiveness. It rediscovers, perhaps, and certainly reaffirms, the concept of guilt, and contrasts the easy physical ability of any animal to go from one locale to another (a thousand mile range, or three moves in six months) with the specially human compass by which guilt moves us to change within. It is a reverent poem about the soul, neglected, which yet abides. Those dead-drunk ducks are dumb to their own beauty. We see it in them, but perhaps we are dumb to *our* own beauty; it is a constant theme in John's work.

John has suffered his art as much as anyone may. In "Homage to Rainer Maria Rilke," Logan has written, "My mere desire shall reach/of itself into rhyme." Readers should see, behind John's deeply emotional, graphic language, and behind the lineated song and muscular vision that has distinguished his poetry since the end of the fifties—behind, that is, the extraordinary sweep of sound he makes, readers should see the keen intelligence which informs it. That is, it has been insufficiently noted how plain smart he is. No poet has testified more eloquently than John to the fact that the heart shares a blood supply with the brain.

October 20, 1983
Iowa City

Courtesy of the Logan family

John Logan, South Bend, Indiana, 1955.

John Logan and The Poetry Seminar

DENNIS SCHMITZ

Late-'50s-early-'60s Chicago was the right place for a young would-be poet who thought the French Surrealists invented modern life: the smog-wooly sky; an old-fashioned machine-boss mayor who spoke oracular prose larded with malapropisms, evasions and nonsensical locutions; the metal and glass Mies van der Rohe buildings like cellular columns that localized light between sooty Chicago-school skyscrapers Sullivan, Wright, Burnam and Adler designed. I was an Iowa boy headed for a Chicago graduate school—I loved it all. I memorized the names and derivations of the landmark buildings, wanting some identification with the excitement.

17

I knew about John Logan from our mutual friend, the poet Ray Roseliep, and through Paul Carroll, who at that time published the early issues of *Big Table*, the magazine (with *Evergreen Review*) which was showing the Beat Generation. I had taken a course from Paul at Loyola University a year or so before I met John. Paul had jollied and teased Chicago poetry into a second coming. None of us who later were included in the Seminar thought what *Poetry* (the *other* Near Northside magazine) was doing was what we wanted to do. Paul's version of poetry was ebullient and cheeky, was the Chicago our age saw. For John, however, speech began in hard listening and total empathy, in congruence. Poetry started far back in odd learning (he knew Latin authors only the Catholics among us recognized) and came out as singing.

John was teaching then at Notre Dame and commuting once a week from South Bend to teach an extension course in writing at the downtown center of the University of Chicago. The future members of the Seminar were drawn chiefly from this class and from Paul's earlier classes at Loyola. Loretta, my future wife, was doing graduate work in French at the main campus of the University of Chicago; one of her classmates in the French program was also in John's class. Loretta invited me to the class one night. A few weeks later, Jordan Miller, who ran a news clipping agency in the Loop area, volunteered his office for Thursday evening meetings of the Seminar (his term, I think). Jordan was a generous entrepreneur of poetry; I don't know how he got my name, but he called.

Jordan had contacted John, I believe, and suggested John's fees (we paid by the week)—he was businesslike. Jordan did all the later incorporation procedures we needed to be able to produce the magazine (*Choice*), to set up readings.

Initially we met around a big table somewhat in the clutter of Jordan's news-clip service. Later, Jordan moved his business to the Fisher Building a block or two away, still in the south Loop area, the elevated tracks themselves just a half-block away. The Fisher Building was a landmark turn-of-the-century design by Burnam; the lobby emphasized the fantasies of manual skill, the black wrought iron that leafed around the elevator column, and a lobby marble so pure the iron railing and grillwork looked etched on it. Jordan took proprietary delight in it.

The sessions were proto-types of the workshop sessions I later taught and saw other poets teaching. John's method was non-directive, not because he was deliberately applying the Rogerian psychology which had an early following then, but because he didn't want to intrude. Shy, skinny and owlish in glasses, with that way of throwing out lines with a follow-through of jaw, his eyes off the paper in front of him, he taught us to read our poems *to* one another, to hear where our voices went wrong in the implied exchange.

John made us believe poems were sounds first, utterances which took color from privacy. He allowed us to make that connection. As a group, we talked and talked; out of the group's push and indecision, John might abstract the few lines to wonder at and spend some time showing us why the lines were good. He was kind. Most of our poems were cheeping and learned bird-calls. He saw the hidden agendas and respected what we had against ourselves as well as what we really wanted to praise but barely could. We evolved under his coaxing. I finally found a peripheral Iowa, not Rimbaud, in my poems a year or two later. Marvin Bell, for example, found a kind of Chassidic yielding. Bill Knott found a persona which allowed him to talk.

The sessions were never long enough. When he didn't stay over in town, John took a late-night Greyhound (cheaper), or the old two-car electric train of the South Shore Line back to South Bend. Always, several of us, insistent and anxious for association, would follow him from the Seminar sessions to Miller's Pub or a similar Loop bar. Or directly into the bluish darkness of the bar under Michigan Ave., at the end of the tunnel that led to the South Shore trains—we all sat knee to knee around a book-size table, spilling drinks and wanting more poetry. The poems collected in *Ghosts of the Heart* and then in *Spring of the Thief* (I had left Chicago to teach in Milwaukee by the time the latter was published) were on dittoed work sheets John tried on us. We heard what he was up to, but we didn't know how to achieve those effects in our poems.

We didn't think of ourselves as a workshop (we didn't know the term), but as an association of writers (probably the way Rosicrucians think of themselves as inheritors of occult powers). We thought of ourselves, I'm sure, as in contention for places in the poetic tradition. Even among ourselves we wanted precedence, though we wanted as well the homogenization 20-year-olds want (the several poets who were older and published, like Beth Fawkes, often must have been amused). I suppose we patronized John too, in a fresh instance of one of his favorite myths, son-against-father, but he was too generous to admit irony in personal relationships. Some of what I recall must be altered by the perspective of twenty-five years—we look smaller now.

The Seminar itself was not monolithic—there were members who attended sessions irregularly, members who came only the first several times, and finally, there was a first Seminar and a second Seminar, sharing some of the same members. Some of the members came in sets: Jim Murphy, who later married Loretta's roommate and with whom I tried a collaborative translation of French poet Jules Supervielle that was cut short by Jim's death in an auto accident, came in with Stu McCarrell and Bob Burleigh. Stu, who owned a small electronics business, contrarily was a loudly-avowed but gentle Marxist—he took the teasing very well.

Bob became a good friend. He was a grad student in Humanities, and later, with me, one of the only PhD students in an odd interdivisional committee at the University of Chicago. I used to go, between classes and the movies at the 63rd Street triple-feature theaters, to the apartment and later the tight little temporary student housing place he and his wife, Bertha, had by the campus. It seemed I always just missed Bob's friend Charlie Simic, whom I didn't meet finally until I lived in California a half-dozen years later.

I also met Marvin Bell at Chicago, in the room where much of the modern poetry collection was housed. He had come there to promote a little magazine he had started. We discovered we were both in the Master's program in English, though we never were in a class together. My friendships with Marvin and with Roger Aplon have been the most sustained of those Seminar relationships.

Because we were transients on our version of Olympus—grad students, business-people (Alice Wolfe owned a beauty salon; Roger did everything from bartending to law research while he went to school)—in a sense John's Chicago time was briefest of any of us—we wanted something more permanent than our own work. It was probably the same impulse I recognized in myself when I memorized the names and locations in the skyline of the classic Chicago architecture. We tried poetry readings by better-known poets: E.E. Cummings read twice under our sponsorship; Robert Lowell and Isabella Gardner read on a twin bill; Kenneth Rexroth read for us at Roosevelt University; poets the University of Chicago Press published (Howard Nemerov, for example) were co-sponsored by us. John, who already *was* a poet and had associations on personal and professional bases with the poets of his generation, Wright, Bly, Ammons, and so on, was the host.

The first reading we did, E.E. Cummings reading at the Great Northern Theater, was one I remember best because Cummings read the day before T.S. Eliot gave the *Poetry* magazine annual benefit reading. (Cummings referred to Eliot as "Tommy"—I was a grad student; I couldn't think of anyone calling Eliot "Tommy," not even his mother, and I suppose that was Cummings' joke.) We thought, naively, that we were sponsoring a rivalry. We wanted a literary event; we wanted Cracker-Jack and prize.

My part in the preparations for the reading was as spear-carrier. I helped Jordan buy the yards and yards of brown burlap we were forced to use as stage backdrop because the management at the Great Northern—a realty agent, I suppose—provided minimal service. The Great Northern was a legitimate theater within a few years of being torn down for a new Mies van der Rohe federal building which would have one property line on Jackson Blvd., where the theater was. We provided some clean-up service for the management; we provided ticket-takers and such. I ran for the (late) silk-screened posters. Others hustled for newspaper reviews, or for a coordination of the reading with an exhibit featuring paintings and drawings by Cummings (this, I think, came with his second reading).

Cummings read to 700-800 people, a monumentally-big audience for those days; the theater seemed full-to-standing-room (it must've been a small theater). He sat alone on the stage behind a small table illuminated by a desk-lamp; the theater was dark enough to make the area of the burlap we could see seem velvety. Cummings read in the slow sing-song we became familiar with in his recordings. It was stagey, but so effective: I was far back in the theater, still circulating, and no one nearby seemed to be breathing.

The meeting with Cummings was important to John, as he indicates in his poem on the death of Cummings. They corresponded, John said, and eventually John began, but never finished, a monograph on Cummings' work. It wasn't a question of influence—John's work was fully-formed, his voice already rich and various. Cummings was a point of spiritual reference but not an orientation. I don't think any other of the readings in the series meant as much to us.

The other way we looked for permanence was with *Choice*, the magazine which became an annual. John thought of it as independent, eclectic, an alternative poetry magazine. He was ready for editorship as a natural exercise of his discrimination. Those were transition days in which little magazines were challenging the dominance of university-based quarterlies.

Paul Carroll, John's friend for a long time, had been publishing *Big Table* for several issues. *Big Table* was in the mold of the best literary journals of the time, from *Evergreen Review* to *Noble Savage* to *Origin*. It had begun as an alternative magazine itself with a first issue which was the material from a *Chicago Review* issue banned by the University because of the "objectionable" work of Burroughs, Ginsberg and others. Paul and the other editors of the *Review*, objecting to the censorship (it was a source of debate in Chicago newspapers at the time), and loss of their initiatives, found money, thank-yous and mixed interest by sponsoring benefit readings by Ginsberg, Corso and other of the banned authors.

Big Table was not the model for *Choice*, but it provided a climate. Maybe John thought *The Fifties* (*The Sixties*, I guess, by that time), edited by his friend Robert Bly, should have been the model—or at least Robert's editorial prerogative might've been the ideal. Robert's magazine was fiercely on the side of principle, had a mission, was independent but was not eclectic. It had all of us reeling from barrages of foreign writers who made us feel effete and provincial, and barrages of editorial iconoclasm that compared to *Big Table's* other mode. John never had the chance, in those early issues, to show what he could do.

Choice (called *Chicago Choice* then) had a fine first issue. The photographer Aaron Siskind, with whom John always has had the best of working relationships, gave John the cover photo (the photo appeared also on the cover of John's selected poems, *Only the Dreamer Can Change the Dream*) for which John had already written the poem "On a

Photograph by Aaron Siskind." John solicited poems from his peers, good poems. We awarded prize money—$100, I think, for the best poem, and a few lesser prizes for follow-up poems. By "we" I mean the magazine's editorial committee—part of the progressive democratization of the Seminar.

I served as first reader for issues one and two, collecting the poems from the magazine's post office box, sorting them, weeding out the obvious rejects. We had editorial meetings after the poems had circulated to the committee. With the second issue, the magazine included portfolios of photos selected by Aaron Siskind. This practice continued for a few issues until funding became difficult, but those issues were as handsome as a magazine could be. Throughout the history of the magazine, John was fortunate to have Roger Aplon's business sense and his managerial ability. Roger was the one who stood strongest behind John then and in the subsequent split with Jordan over control of the magazine (and in some senses, over leadership of the Seminar). *Choice* survived as an annual (sometimes irregular bi-annual, like *The Sixties*)—one of the best literary magazines of those days—because of Roger's support for John.

I have much for which to thank John—beside the nagging urge to write poetry—John helped me with my first teaching job. When I teach now, I sometimes find myself uttering Logan-isms. John must have affected all of us similarly; he taught us self-amazement—not self-pity, self-indulgence.

I haven't seen Dave Gilman, Alice, Irene Keller since then, and very little of Dave Cohen (the names are still all there: Myrtle Chamberlin, Jim Bonk, Alan Goldfarb, Carolyn Siskind), but I carry around some of their lines. Jessie Kachmar, Naomi Lazard, Bob Burleigh, Stu, Marjorie, Bill Hunt and Bill Knott I saw again a few years ago when the University of Illinois in Chicago sponsored a three-day conference devoted to the work of that generation of Chicago poets, ultimately centering on John's contribution. We exchanged poems again—poets more now because we cared less that we were. John had been successful in that too: I loved these people as much as I loved what I had been with them.

Only the Dreamer Can Change the Dream / John Logan

SELECTED POEMS

The Picnic

It is the picnic with Ruth in the spring.
Ruth was third on my list of seven girls
But the first two were gone (Betty) or else
Had someone (Ellen has accepted Doug).
Indian Gully the last day of school;
Girls make the lunches for the boys too.
I wrote a note to Ruth in algebra class
Day before the test. She smiled, and nodded.
We left the cars and walked through the young corn
The shoots green as paint and the leaves like tongues
Trembling. Beyond the fence where we stood
Some wild strawberry flowered by an elm tree
And Jack-in-the-pulpit was olive ripe.
A blackbird fled as I crossed, and showed
A spot of gold or red under its quick wing.
I held the wire for Ruth and watched the whip
Of her long, striped skirt as she followed.
Three freckles blossomed on her thin, white back
Underneath the loop where the blouse buttoned.
We went for our lunch away from the rest,
Stretched in the new grass, our heads close
Over unknown things wrapped up in wax papers.
Ruth tried for the same, I forgot what it was,
And our hands were together. She laughed,
And a breeze caught the edge of her little
Collar and the edge of her brown, loose hair
That touched my cheek. I turned my face in-
to the gentle fall. I saw how sweet it smelled.
She didn't move her head or take her hand.
I felt a soft caving in my stomach
As at the top of the highest slide
When I had been a child, but was not afraid,
And did not know why my eyes moved with wet
As I brushed her cheek with my lips and brushed

Her lips with my own lips. She said to me
Jack, Jack, different than I had ever heard,
Because she wasn't calling me, I think,
Or telling me. She used my name to
Talk in another way I wanted to know.
She laughed again and then she took her hand;
I gave her what we both had touched—can't
Remember what it was, and we ate the lunch.
Afterward we walked in the small, cool creek
Our shoes off, her skirt hitched, and she smiling,
My pants rolled, and then we climbed up the high
Side of Indian Gully and looked
Where we had been, our hands together again.
It was then some bright thing came in my eyes,
Starting at the back of them and flowing
Suddenly through my head and down my arms
And stomach and my bare legs that seemed not
To stop in feet, not to feel the red earth
Of the Gully, as though we hung in a
Touch of birds. There was a word in my throat
With the feeling and I knew the first time
What it meant and I said, it's beautiful.
Yes, she said, and I felt the sound and word
In my hand join the sound and word in hers
As in one name said, or in one cupped hand.
We put back on our shoes and socks and we
Sat in the grass awhile, crosslegged, under
A blowing tree, not saying anything.
And Ruth played with shells she found in the creek,
As I watched. Her small wrist which was so sweet
To me turned by her breast and the shells dropped
Green, white, blue, easily into her lap,
Passing light through themselves. She gave the pale
Shells to me, and got up and touched her hips
With her light hands, and we walked down slowly
To play the school games with the others.

Lines on His Birthday

I was born on a street named Joy
of which I remember nothing,
but since I was a boy
I've looked for its lost turning.
Still I seem to hear my mother's cry
echo in the street of joy.
She was sick as Ruth for home
when I was born. My birth
took away my father's wife
and left me half
my life. Christ will my remorse
be less when my father's dead?
Or more. As Lincoln's minister of war
kept the body of his infant boy
in a silver coffin on his desk,
so I keep
in a small heirloom box of teak
the picture of my living father.
Or perhaps it is an image of myself
dead in this box she held?
I know her milk like ivory blood
still runs in my thick veins
and leaves in me an almost
lickerish taste for ghosts:
my mother's wan face,
full brown hair, the mammoth breast
death cuts off at the bone—
to which she draws her bow
again, brazen Amazon,
and aiming deadly as a saint
shoots her barb
of guilt into my game heart.

January 23, 1961

27

Spring of the Thief

But if I look the ice is gone from the lake
and the altered air
no longer fills with the small
terrible bodies of the snow.
Only once these late winter weeks
the dying flakes
fell instead as manna or as wedding rice
blooming in the light
about the bronze Christ
and the Thieves. There these three
still hang, more than man-
sized and heavier than life
on a hill over the lake
where I walk
this Third Sunday of Lent.
I come from Mass
melancholy at its ancient story
of the unclean ghost
a man thought he'd lost.
It came back into his well-swept house
and at the final state that man
was worse than he began.
Yet again today
there is the faintest edge of green
to trees about St. Joseph's Lake.
Ah God if our confessions show contempt
because we let them free us of our guilt
to sin again
forgive us still . . . before the leaves . . .
before the leaves have formed
you can glimpse the Christ and Thieves
on top of the hill. One of them was saved.

That day the snow had seemed to drop like grace
upon the four of us,
or like the peace of intercourse,
suddenly I wanted to confess—
or simply talk.
I paid a visit to the mammoth Sacred Heart
Church, and found it shut.
Who locked him out or in?
The name of God is changing in our time.
What is his winter name?
Where was his winter home?
Oh I've kept my love to myself before.
Even those ducks weave down the shore
together, drunk with hope
for the April water. One spring festival
near here I stripped and strolled
through a rain filled field.
Spread eagled on the soaking earth
I let the rain
move its audible little hands
gently on my skin . . . let the dark rain
raise up my love.
But why? I was alone
and no one saw how ardent I grew.
And when I rolled naked in the snow one night
as St. Francis with his Brother Ass
or a hard bodied Finn
I was alone. Underneath
the howling January moon
I knelt and dug my fist
full of the cold winter sand
and rubbed and
hid my manhood under it.
Washed up at some ancient or half-heroic shore
I was ashamed that I was naked there.

Before Nausicaä and the saints. Before myself.
But who took off my coat? Who put it on?
Who drove me home?
Blessed be sin if it teaches men shame.
Yet because of it we cannot talk
and I am separated from myself.
So what is all this reveling in snow and rain?
Or in the summer sun when the heavy gold
body weeps with joy or grief or love?
When we speak of God, is it God we speak of?
Perhaps his winter home
is in that field where I rolled or ran . . .
this hill where once the snow
fell serene as rain.
Oh I have walked around the lake
when I was not alone—
sometimes with my wife have seen these swans
dip down their necks
graceful as a girl, showering white and wet!
I've seen their heads delicately turn.
Have gone sailing with my quiet, older son.
And once on a morning walk
a student who had just come back
in fall found a perfect hickory shell
among the bronze and red
leaves and purple flowers of the time
and put its white bread into my hand.
Ekelöf said there is a freshness
nothing can destroy in us—
not even we ourselves.
Perhaps that
Freshness is the changed name of God.
Where all the monsters also hide
I bear him in the ocean of my blood

and in the pulp of my enormous head.
He lives beneath the unkempt potter's grass
of my belly and chest.
I feel his terrible, aged heart
moving under mine . . . can see the shadows
of the gorgeous light
that plays at the edges of his giant eye . . .
or tell the faint press and hum
of his eternal pool of sperm.
Like sandalwood! *Like sandalwood*
the righteous man
perfumes the axe that falls on him.
The cords of elm, of cedar oak and pine
will pile again in fall.
The ribs and pockets of the barns will swell.
Winds and fires in the field rage
and again burn out each
of the ancient roots.
Again at last the late November snow
will fill those fields, change this hill,
throw these figures in relief
and raining on them
will transform
the bronze Christ's brow and cheek,
the white face and thigh of the thief.

March-April 1962

Three Moves

Three moves in six months and I remain
the same.
Two homes made two friends.
The third leaves me with myself again.
(We hardly speak.)
Here I am with tame ducks
and my neighbors' boats,
only this electric heat
against the April damp.
I have a friend named Frank—
the only one who ever dares to call
and ask me, "How's your soul?"
I hadn't thought about it for a while,
and was ashamed to say I didn't know.
I have no priest for now.
Who
will forgive me then. Will you?
Tame birds and my neighbors' boats.
The ducks honk about the floats . . .
They walk dead drunk onto the land and grounds
iridescent blue and black and green and brown.
They live on swill
our aged houseboats spill.
But still they are beautiful.
Look! The duck with its unlikely beak
has stopped to pick
and pull
at the potted daffodil.
Then again they sway home
to dream
bright gardens of fish in the early night.
Oh these ducks are all right.
They will survive.
But I am sorry I do not often see them climb.
Poor sons-a-bitching ducks.
You're all fucked up.
What do you do that for?
Why don't you hover near the sun anymore?

Afraid you'll melt?
These foolish ducks lack a sense of guilt,
and so all their multi-thousand-mile range
is too short for the hope of change.

Seattle, April 1965

Poem, Slow to Come,
on the Death of Cummings
(1894-1962)

*"I care more about strawberries
than about death."*

"Herr, es ist Zeit."

1

Lord, it is time now. The winter
has gone on and gone on.
Spring was brief.
Summer blasts the roots of trees and weeds
again, and you are dead
almost a year. I am sorry for my fear,
but you were father's age, and you were fond;
I saw it in your eyes when I put you on the plane.
Today it is too late to write
or visit as you asked.
I feel I let you die.
I chose the guilt over all the joy.
Now I know you cannot hear me say,
and so my elegy is for me.

2

I knew your serenity. Compassion.
Integrity. But I could not feel your death
until I visited your wife.
She is haggard with the burden of your loss.
I wish I had not come

before, when you were there,
and she served currant jam
on toast and you poured brandy in the tea
and laughed, slapping your thigh
and hopped, like a small, happy boy,
about your newly painted Village place.
Now the color on your walls and hers
is not fresh. It has peeled with the falling
of your flesh. Your paintings in the house already date,
especially the soft, romantic nude you did
(although I love it best):
Her dark hair full to hips,
girlish, unsucked breasts,
rather pensive belly, skin
a lucid gold or red like a faded blush.
Her beautiful, jet feminine bush.
And the limbs you made, thin with their own light,
with the glow of that other world:
Women. Estlin, your poems are full of love—
you wanted to know that other world
while you were still alive.
All poets do. All men. All gods.
Inside a woman we search for the lost wealth
of our self. Marcel says,
"Death is not a problem to be solved.
It is a mystery to be entered into."
Then you have what you wanted, Estlin,
for Death is a woman,
and there is no more need for a poem.
Your death fulfills and it is strong.
I wish I had not died when I was so young.

3

Your last summer at your farm
like a young man again you cut down
an aging, great New England oak.
Oh you are big and you would not start to stoop
even on that absolute day.
I feel you are a giant, tender gnome.
Like a child you came home
tired, and you called your wife
asking to be clean. Still tall you tossed
the odd body of your sweaty clothes
to her down, down the ancient stairs,
and it was there as the ghost
tumbled, suddenly you were struck
brilliant to your knees! Your back
bent. You wrapped your lean,
linen arms close around your life
naked as before our birth,
and began to weave away from earth
uttering with a huge, awkward, torn cry
the terrible, final poetry.

July 1963-August 1964

On the Death of Keats

Lines for Those Who Drown Twice

I am recommended not even to read poetry,
much less to write it. I wish I had even a
little hope.

Send me just the words "good night," to put
under my pillow.
—Keats to Fanny Brawne

I do not care a straw for foreign flowers.
The simple flowers of our spring are what I
want to see again.
—Keats to James Rice

1

The last month in your little Roman house
your eyes grew huge and bright as those
a gentle animal opens to the night.
Although you could not write or read
you were calmed by the thought of books
beside your bed.
(Jeremy Taylor your favorite one.
Plato and the comic Don.)
"How long is this posthumous life of mine
to last," you said.
What is a poet without breath enough?
The doctor made you swallow cupfuls of your blood
when it came up
out of your rotten lungs again.

Your study of medicine
made you suffer more the movements
of your death. One tiny fish
and a piece of black bread
to control the blood
every day you died. You starved for food
and air. For poetry. For love.
(Yet you could not read her
letters for the pain.)
One night you saw a candle flame
beautifully pass across a thread from one
taper to start another.
All month you heard the sound of water
weeping in the Bernini fount.
You asked your friend to lift you up,
and died so quietly he thought you slept.
They buried you with Shelley
at a cold February dawning
beside his drowned heart
which had survived a life
and death of burning.

2

Ruth and I visited your grave
in Rome's furious August rain.
The little old Protestant plot
beyond the pyramid the Romans, home from Egypt, made
in the middle of the city.
All the names are English,
which nobody knows or nods to
in the awful noise and light. Nobody speaks.

This rain springs from ancient seas
that burst
behind the bones of my face
and wash in salt tides
over the small shells of my eyes.
Since my birth
I've waited for the terror of this place.
The gravekeeper in his hooded black
rubber cloak
wades ahead of us toward your tomb.
The streams that shape and change
along the tender's rubber back
light in the thunder flash
into grotesque slits of eyes.
They see my fright. Ruth's hand
is cold in my cold hand.
You, Keats, and Shelley and Ruth
and I all drown again
away from home
in this absurd rain of Rome,
as you once drowned in your own phlegm,
and I in my poem. I am afraid.
The gravekeeper waits.
He raises his black arm.
He gestures in the black rain. The sky
moans long.
His hooded eyes fire again!
Suddenly I can read the stone
which publishes your final line:
Its date is the birthday of my brother!
"Here lies one whose name was writ on water."
Oh Keats, the violet. The violet. The violet
was your favorite flower.

Suzanne

You make us want to stay alive, Suzanne,
the way you turn

your blonde head.
The way you curve your slim hand

toward your breast.
When you drew your legs

up, sitting by the fire,
and let your bronze hair

stream about your knees
I could see the grief

of the girl in your eyes.
It touched the high,

formal bones of your face.
Once I heard it in your lovely voice

when you sang—
the terrible time of being young.

Yet you bring us joy with your
self, Suzanne, wherever you are.

And once, although I wasn't here,
you left three roses on my stair.

One party night when you were high
you fled barefoot down the hall,

the fountain of your laughter
showering through the air.

"Chartreuse," you chanted
(the liqueur you always wanted),

"I have yellow chartreuse hair!"
Oh it was a great affair.

You were the most exciting person there.
Yesterday when I wasn't here

again,
you brought a blue, porcelain

egg to me—
colored beautifully

for the Russian Easter.
Since then, I have wanted to be your lover,

but I have only touched your shoulder
and let my fingers brush your hair,

because you left three roses on my stair.

The Search

But for whom do I look?
The whole long night you will see me walk
or maybe during the day
watch me pass by.
But I do not wander—
it is a search. For I stop here,
or here, wherever people gather.
Depot, restaurant, bar.
But whom do I seek?
You will see me coming back
perhaps at dawn. Sometimes
the faces seem like tombs.
I have tried to read the names
so long my eyes darken in their graves
of bone. (The bodies of our eyes
lie side by side
and do not touch.)
But for whom do I look? My search
is not for wife, daughter or for son
for time to time
it has taken me from them.
Or has wrenched me from my friend:
I will abruptly leave him,
and I do not go home.
For whom do I seek? Out of what fear?
It is not for queers,
for my search leads me from their bars.
It is not for whores,
since I reject their wares,

or another time may not.
Then for whom do I look?
When I was young I thought
I wanted (yearned for) older age.
Now I think I hunt with so much rage
that I will risk or lose
family or friends for the ghost of my youth.
Thus I do not know for what I look.
Father? Mother?
The father who will be the mother?
Sister who will be the brother?
Often I hunt in the families of others—
until hope scatters.
I will call up friend or student at night
or I will fly
to see them—will bask and heal in the warm
places of their homes.
And I must not be alone
no matter what needs be done,
for then my search is ended.
So now the panicked thumbs of my poem pick
through the grill. They poke
the lock
and put out a hand and then an arm.
The limbs of my poems
come within your reach.
Perhaps it is you whom I seek.

Only the Dreamer
Can Change the Dream

Riding on his bike
in the fall
or spring Fel-
lini-like twilight
or dawn, the boy
                    is moved in some way
he does not understand.
A huge gray or green, long porched house
(he's partly color-blind)
crowns a low hill: rise-
s silent as a ship does
before him.
The vision makes him yearn
inside himself. It makes him mourn.
So he cries
            as he rides
                        about the town.
He knows there are other great homes
and other beautiful streets
nearby. But they are not his.
He turns back.
                  He gets off his bike
and picks
            up three fragments of unfinished pine
adrift on the green
                    (or gray) lawn
thinking—hoping—that perhaps
there is something some place he can fix.

Poem:

Tears, Spray, and Steam

(In Memoriam: Eric Barker)

1

Peering, stung,
            bleared, hung-
over and lame,
through the waves of spray,
I feel somewhat
            panicky,
weird, about my sweat-
            ing body.
For where do we and our vapors end?
Where does the bath begin?

Strange to be able to see through the steam
(but satisfying to the point of calm,
like the vision of the perfect, new born)
for the first time
the whole,
            beautiful body of a friend.

Like a god
            damned eternal thief
of heat,
      clouds
wreathing round
your black, bearded head,
belly, limbs and your sex
(but no piercing eagle about,
yet)
you lie flat on your back
on the rock
            ledge bench in the bath,
Promethean in your black
                  wrath.

2

In our nun's or monk's
                    black

rubber hoods
(lace-paper coifs
                    just visible at the tops
of our heads),
as if about to pray,
and black rubber coats
                    to our feet
because of the spray,
we walk the Niagara Tunnel.
You can tell
            almost for sure
which ones the kids are,
but you can't tell men from women here.
Unsexed in these catacombs we watch
for the asperges of the bath.
The damp walls bleed rice.
All dark, all si-
                    lent, we all pass.
We bow, each to each,
and some,
            not only young,
give the ancient kiss of peace,
standing in the alcoves again.
We reach for rain.
The Falls' spray touches each of us.
The glass
            over our eyes
                        weeps.

Cheeks
        are wet. Lips.
Even our teeth if our mouths gape.
We are caress-
                ed with wetness

all about our cloaks,
and we sway
                and float
broken out in a dark sweat,
complex, prodigious:
female, white, male, black, lay, religious.
At last we all
                peer out the stone holes
at the back of the Falls
and see nothing but The Existential Wall:
water roaring out of the hidden hills.
Power passes us, detached,
                        abstract,
except for this cold steam
that licks and teases
                until at last
we turn our drenched, glistening backs.

        3
Aging, still
        agile
poet Eric Barker,
who has been coming
(I almost said springing)
back here
        for many years,
and I and two friends
strip at the still springs
with their
        full smell of sulphur—
here where bodies and warm water
are moon- and candle-lit, wind woven,
in a shallow cavern
                open
to the heaving, iridescent sea
near
    Big Sur,

and we invade the great,
                    Roman bath
intimidat-
ing the Esalen teacher with his small class:
three naked girls in three corners of the big tub—
he, their leader,
                    in the other.
The candles waver
as the class takes cover
                    and the mad teacher
leaves with one student to find
a night watchman, leaving behind
the others:
            one of them   •
already slithers
in a smaller tub with one of our friends.
The third girl now fully dressed—
and for the moment repress-
ed—stares
            at the rest of us
lolling and floating our masculine flowers
as we give a naked reading of William Butler
Yeats to each other
                    (taking care not
to get the book wet)
and then we read to her
as she begins to listen.
                    So she too strips and
slips into the fourth corner,
becomes for a moment our teacher.
Her breasts come alive in the water.
Yeats
      will wait
and Keats—for Barker, with whom
we have been drinking wine
all afternoon
knows
      all the Odes
                  by heart

as well as many
                bawdy songs:
  "My long
        delayed erection,"
he'd recited, laughing,
"rises in the wrong direction."
But he too is silent
for the while, and
                sits stately,
buoyed by the
                water: its movement
makes his white
body hair seem to sprout.
Soon,
      we begin
              to say the poems again
and to touch each other—
                the older
man, me,
the boys and the girls read-
ing over the sea's
sounds
      by the candles'
light and the moon bright, burgeoning,
shin-
    ing time to time
                as
the clouds pass.
              In this gently flash-
ing light then
we all leave the tubs and run
dripping down the shore
together before
          any others come—
as hostile teacher, watchman.
But in that warm spring
water which we briefly left, everything
                eventually heals:
for, by
      the sea

it flows out of these ancient, California hills,
which are the trans-
                    formed,
giant body of a once
powerful, feather, bone and turquoise-adorned
Indian Prince,
                    and the sulphur is the changed
sharp incense
                    he burned daily as he chanted
year and year over for the sick young princess—
who took her loveliness
from the many-colored, fragrant trees
and the flickering sea.
Finally, unable to help,
                    he thought,
the tawny-skinned prince
died of his grief,
and his body became this mount-
ain. And everybody here who comes together
                                        in belief
is somehow bound, bathed,
                    and made
whole, e-
        ven as was she
by this gradual, glinting water,
the prince's continual tears for his sister.

So, when we return a little later
from our dance along the open shore
we find the Esalen
                    teacher there again,
and the watchman,
each with a woman.
They wait
            in that gentle, lunatic light for us.
They smile as they undress.
Eric Barker takes a leak,
begins reciting Keats,
and we all bathe and sing together
in the new waters of brother, sister.

THE BRIDGE OF CHANGE

POEMS 1974-1980

JOHN LOGAN

Poem for My Brother

Blue's my older brother's color. Mine is brown, you see.
So today I bought this ring
of gold and lapis lazuli flecked with a bright bronze.
His blue is the light hue of his eyes. Brown's the color
of our dead mother's long hair,
which fell so beautifully about her young shoulders
in the picture, and of my own eyes (I can't tell hers).
I loved my brother, but never quite knew what to think.
For example, he would beat
me up as soon as the folks
left the house, and I would cry big, loud feminine tears.
He was good at sports and played football, and so instead
I was in the marching band.
My brother stole rubbers from the store and smoked cigars
and pipes, which made me sick. But
once we swam together in
the Nishnabotna river
near home, naked, our blue overalls piled together
by the water, their copper
buttons like the bronze glints in my ring. I remember
once when I was very young
I looked deep into a pool
of blue water—we had no mirror—and I was so
amazed I looked over my shoulder, for I did not
imagine it was me, caught
in that cerulean sky.
Thinking it was someone other, I tell you I con-
fused myself with my brother!
Nothing goes with gold, but I can see in this rich blue
stone the meeting of our clothes like the touching of hands
when he taught me to hold my fishing pole well and wound
up the reel for me. You know
blue is the last of the primary colors to be named.

Why, some primitive societies still have no word
for it except "dark." It's associated with black:
in the night my brother and I
would play at games that neither of us could understand.
But this is not a confession; it is a question.
We've moved apart and don't write,
and our children don't even know their own cousin!
So, I would have you know I
want this ring to *engage* us
in reconciliation.
Blue is the color of the heart.
I won't live forever. Is it too late now to be
a brother to my brother?
Let the golden snake bend round
again to touch itself and
all at once burst into azure!

—1974

Grace

We suffer from the repression of the sublime.
                —Roberto Assagioli

This artist's sculptured, open box of mahogany
(ivory white inside) is strung
with vertical and horizontal layers of mus-
ical wires that sing when struck, and bits of bright garnet
rock tremble where they intersect.
These gems flash in the candle light,
and before me all my beloved childhood looms up
in the humming levels, each one deeper than the other.
I tip this sculpted box and my child laughs and moves there
in his own time. You'll hear me moan:
Oh, you will hear me moan with all the old, sure pleasure
of what I'd thought I'd lost come back again.
Why, we have never left our home!
On the leather lace fixed about my neck, blue, yellow,
red and black African trading beads begin to glow:
their colors all weave and newly flow
together like translucent and angelic worms.
And beneath these my neck is as alive with gentle,
white bees as is a woman's breast.
Beside and in the light river
figures come on stage exactly
as they are needed. I tell you, I conduct my own
act! A boy poses so youthfully,
so beautifully, his slim arms a graceful arrow
over his small, brown head, and he dives!
Limbs and body push supple as a whole school of fish.
And then his vacant place is taken by another—
a man dressed in denim and in boots of red rubber.

He is wrenched from the shore and pulled
through the fresh, bright stream by a kid
who tugs on one of his hands and holds a fishing rod.
And, too, this man is dragged in the opposite direction
by a red dog on a leash shaking his wet
great coat into the stippled light.
That man just sashayed: he zigzagged
this way and that. The man is me!

A bluejay does a dance for us!
He hops beside a tree that rises inside of me.
He half-glides, his iridescent,
blue back striking like a brush
of Gauguin on the bare canvas of the air and then:
he flies! leaving behind him a small, perfect feather,
which I find shades from blue to brown—
my brother's color into mine.
Now in the space the diver and the booted fellow
left, my brother and I are there
fishing together, our poles glinting in the water.
My mouth moves. My eyes are alive!
I cry to my brother with joy.
For that bluejay was a messenger of what I want!

Gregory my friend and guide on this voyage seems benign.
He brushes my chest and my stretched,
naked arms open to the sun
with a branch of the fragrant pine.
"Be healed," he chants with each glancing
stroke. "Be healed." The needles prick my skin back into life,
and I go down to bathe my feet in the stream. The veins
form a light, mottled web along my white ankle.

I feel my kinship with the pine,
the jay, the luminescent stream
and with him—or is it with *her*,
the Mother? Gregory, my oracle, my teacher.
He leans there in the door of our tent by the river,
his face glowing, hair long and shining as a woman's,
his belly fat with life—pregnant with the two of us:
my brother and I, unborn twins who lie entangled
in each other's developing
limbs. Soon we will be born! He and I will taste of milk
for the very first time! And taste of strawberry pop
and of bright bananas. And we will eat, my brother
and I, a great, shining, autumn-red apple fallen
from our father's tree as if from the long sky, and *you*
too will taste this apple with us
for we all have the same mother, and her name is Grace.

Assateague

Tamar and Royce are in love.
They run up the beach and give
each other a hand. I walk
behind and brood. I'll try my luck:

Grey the beach at Assateague.
Grey the sky and grey the sea.
A white heron whirls off now
and a spider crab comes out

of its hole, scuds swiftly back
having sensed a big mistake.
I find a white plastic bit
I had thought was a devil fish.

The washed-up wood of old ships
breaks the sand, with shells like coins
lost from Spanish galleons
that used to try these awful seas.

One ship torn up on the reef
left a heritage of dwarf
wild ponies from centuries
before, and still two herds of these

roam the shores and live on marsh
grasses. The round-up is harsh
yearly, decimates the herds
driven before the waves and winds:

They swim across the channel
goaded by the boys and men
and up the beach into pens
pattering up over moist sands

and dashing the placid salt
pools into myriad drops.
Roped and with spirits broken,
the ponies are driven inland

and for the rest of their bound
lives they yearn for salt and sedge
they fed on under the ridge
of snow along the island edge

as we yearn for our childhood
or the love we never had
or else had but could not keep
until we came to Assateague.

for Michael and Robin Waters
—1978

Lines for an Unknown Lover

I desire to hold in my heart
(which is shaped like a child's fist) the thin stems of feelings
no one has ever felt. They'll burst
in great bouquets your touch gathers
up from the unlikely roots of my fingers and toes:
sudden, resonant, color full—
the blues, reds and golds will damage the bulb of my eye
beautifully. And I will give you back a caress
you can tell in the delicate tip of your eyelash,
feel echoing quiet at the
first and then more stridently in the hidden fronds weav-
ing upwards toward the bright trellis of your belly.
Listen to the sound! It is dis-
sonant above the musical
ground bass, the passacaglia of your humming sex.
And when we join, all these colors will match all these sounds
and the broad strings I bear in the arched rainbow of my
body will bury themselves, well, nearly noisily
in the scudding clouds of your breast.
Your breast's light lights up your unknown face.

60

Elegy for Dylan Thomas

1

In the Welsh town of Laugharne across the way from the Brown
Inn your wife Caitlin lived (by half her life): she had brought
your body back from where you died—
the White Horse Tavern in New York.
The old pub at Brown's stays open
long as the patrons want, for Laugharne is a little town.
The people—even the bar-keep—stay awake and drink
and talk of you (now famous in this place), and they tell
the tale of Caitlin on the way to the funeral:
she was late because she came across the street and cried
and drank the warm pints of bitter just as you had done.
The funeral procession weaved,
lurched up the street toward the Church.

2

In October, month of your birth,
my friend and I took the night train
from London's Paddington Station past the sleep-tossed towns
and the sheep nudging gently on the hills,
through Swansea town where you were born
and came to Laugharne—where you wrote your last and best poems—
to follow your funeral steps.
But first we looked where you had lived—
saw the Laugharne Castle ("brown as owls"),
your herons standing on one leg tentative as life
in the rich, reaching waters of the estuary,
black as funeral priests against
the sun, black as the crow-capped Sir John's Hill where we walked
with you up the thigh of childhood
toward the crown and vision of age you never reached—
although in poems you clowned how it would be to be old.

We stared through the glass in the small door of the house
where you wrote, imagining we could see manuscripts
strewn across the floor and the circular stains from beer
bottles interspersed, like abstract geometric spooks,
among the books you loved: Hardy, Hopkins and Traherne
and the pictures pinned to walls: Lawrence, Whitman, Blake,
and the few nudes you always had.
This shack where you worked seems precarious on the ledge
above the sea, like the boathouse
nearby at the end of its breakneck of rocks on stilts
where you lived with your wife and kids
and watched the tides lap at the house's stone foundations.
But these places are more durable than our life. They
are more durable than our life.

3
The bright cobbled streets wind briefly,
beautiful, up the leaf-strewn hills of Laugharne. (Trees tell truth.)
For such a tiny town, it is well supplied with pubs
for there are seven, and my friend
and I visit all of them (after you did, Dylan).
We sit at the very window table where you drank
in Brown's and we look through the lace
across the way to Caitlin's house.
We think, are we ready for the trip to Trinity Church?
We decide we are and set out.
But it is hard to feel the funeral, hear the dirge
this sun-filled day (once you wrote of "the core of the sun's
bush") as we pass the white, green, yellow neat Welsh houses
and the hall where again tonight
performers from Swansea will act
your final work, and your books are all on sale—
because it's Dylan Thomas Festival!
But as the Churchyard gate swings shut
I feel my heart stepped on like a stone in the Church walk.

Here there are centuries of dead, for the Church is old,
and the ghosts of funeral processions pass and pass
as the two of us near the little, white wooden cross
that marks your grave, Dylan Thomas.
Now we stand at its narrow foot.
We know your body is as close to us as we are
to each other. My friend begins silently to weep
for you, and for him and me, but suddenly I see
your image stand before us there
among the gray, half-leaning graves of the ancient dead,
all of them. Dylan, you are buried up to the waist
in the yellow leaves of autumn!
Should I say, perhaps buried *only* up to the waist,
for despite the melancholy in your eyes, your art,
which you worked beneath "singing light,"
will leave you more unburied yet?
No. That is a trick of the heart.
Beneath my living feet, I know
your heavy body rots,
and I shake like these drying aster stems among the tombs.
Why, even the gravestones tremble
at the touch of time. So I will touch my friend once more
for the solace of the living—
and for the solaces of art,
whose mysteries deepen in the grave,
I will read your poems again.

for Joseph Stroud
—1978

Papa's House, Son's Room

1

In Key West, poinciana trees bloom flamboyant red
before the leaves begin, and here in Hemingway's yard
the bare Lenten tree soon will bloom
bright as the blood from Papa's head,
red as the bricks from the wall he built around the house—
carting them home from the torn trolley track on Duvall
Street. Red as the blast from the safe
after his death—where his wife found the undone ms.
of *Islands in The Stream:* the father, his friends and sons:
their unfinished relationships.

2

I see the little boys sit
(Gregory, the younger, I knew)
at a small table between the dining room
and the kitchen—its appliances raised six inches
from the floor so great Papa could clean and cook his catch.
Those little boys sat and heard their parents eat at what
a table!—Eighteenth-Century Spanish, with storage space
for the gentlemen's swords fixed at the back of the chairs!
And one of Pauline's beloved chandeliers above—
this one hand-blown Venetian glass.
Over the black Greek mantle, a mounted gnu, trophy
from that extraordinary father's first safari.
The small boys played around Pauline's crouching crystal cats,
which poise on a table in the parlor and squint down
at the strolling or lolling fifty Hemingway cats.
Still the descendants scud through, each with six inbred toes.

3

Picasso's gift ceramic cat
overlooks, from on top a tall mysteriously tiled cabinet,
the master bedroom with its stiff midwife's stool and birthing chair
positioned at opposite walls.
That labor chair Papa took down to Sloppy Joe's Bar
and bore stories inside his head,
while he sat with friends all afternoon and drank his beer.
His boys fished and swam at the tiny beach
the days Papa did not take them out on the boat.
His buddy, the bartender's son, said of him:
"Nobody could keep up with him—if you didn't get a strike,
you drank to change your luck. If you got that strike, you drank
to celebrate!"

4

        Hemingway not only brought that chair,
he salvaged something from the bar:
he toted a cracked, old urinal home on his back!
He wanted to water the cats!
Pauline was shocked and mad a while,
then solved the problem with glued French tile!
Papa never went to the bar
until he'd worked all morning at home in his study—
after breakfast crossing from the upstairs veranda
on a frail bridge across the yard
to the loft of the rebuilt barn,
breathing sun-warmed tropical plants
he'd trucked and back-packed and sweated
to plant from all over the Keys
to make a garden for the muse.
(But to the boys it must have seemed he reared a jungle!)

5

Those weird chairs and the gifted cat
in the bedroom were made quite small
by the custom king-size bed, its broken-hinged head-board
fashioned from a mahogany gate he'd brought from Spain.
How did those young brothers feel in their plain room beside?
But now their small beds are broken down, and Gregory's
gnarled head-board leans against the larger one of the maid.

6

Gregory. His Catholic books
(there was only school through eighth grade)
are now in a glass case in his room, and the priest is dead.
The priest was an old friend of his Dad's, whose own cases
overgrow that childhood room, filled with pictures of *him*
and *his* friends, and souvenirs from all over the world.

7

Gregory. I knew some of his later history
when I was his teacher at a school in Maryland.
He was a smart and beautiful man.
We would have coffee after Mass,
talk of his restlessness with college and with himself.
He never spoke of his father
and, unlike his brother, did not become a hunter.
He didn't finish the term. I haven't seen him since.
It's thirty years, but today our lives breathe together
briefly as I stand in your parents' house and your room
and wait (Oh, it will happen again soon)
for the Lenten tree to bloom.

Believe It

There is a two-headed goat, a four-winged chicken
and a sad lamb with seven legs
whose complicated little life was spent in Hopland,
California. I saw the man with doubled eyes
who seemed to watch in me my doubts about my spirit.
Will it snag upon this aging flesh?

There is a strawberry that grew
out of a carrot plant, a blade
of grass that lanced through a thick rock,
a cornstalk nineteen-feet-two-inches tall grown by George
Osborne of Silome, Arkansas.
There is something grotesque growing in me I cannot tell.

It has been waxing, burgeoning, for a long time.
It weighs me down like the chains of the man of Lahore
who began collecting links on his naked body
until he crawled around the town carrying the last
thirteen years of his life six-hundred-seventy pounds.
Each link or each lump in me is an offense against love.

I want my own lit candle lamp buried in my skull
like the Lighthouse Man of Chungking,
who could lead the travelers home.
Well, I am still a traveler and I don't know where
I live. If my home is here, inside my breast,
light it up! And I will invite you in as my first guest.

> *for Tina Logan*
> *After visiting the Believe It or Not Museum*
> *with her in San Francisco*
> *—1980*

from

Manhattan Movements

Poems by

John Logan

The Transformation

Dissonant music of the night.
Two o'clock. The ancient dogs cry.
Seventeen year old Harry homing from a party
hauls a radio that sounds the harsh tones of the young.
Joseph soughing, sighing on the couch twists in his sleep.
Poor Joseph sleeps off who knows what.
But I am heedless, for tonight
I was warmed by my father's touch.
I want to tell you how it was.
After Bartok at the symphony
Renée and I found high in the sky a good spot and talked
out of our growing, friendly love
far above the buildings shining attractive at night
in Waikiki: Suddenly a strangely dressed lady
(I can't tell you where she came from)
stopped at our small table and sought to take our picture.
Renée and I first said no to her, then by some quirk
or other I simply ran after.
We moved our black rattan chairs close together, smiled and
twice we let her flash our picture.
We had another drink, chatted
and with a slight edge of expectation we waited.
After an undetermined time
the mythical lady returned
and we were amazed to find quite fabulous photos!
Renée was radiant in a dress now trimmed with stars,
and as for me I had lost weight
and showed the true bones of my face.
For the first time I knew I looked like my father's son.
I am fifty-eight. Let those dogs
of the moon bay again tonight,
the young stage their noisy parties
and Joseph sleep his obscure sleep.
I am pleased because I see I have my father's face.

The Piano Scholar

(for Aunt Gladys Woods)

My grandfather Remmers was a German immigrant
trained in classical piano,
and he gave instruction to the richer town ladies.
He would ride his rounds on horseback,
carry with him a horn baton
and rap on his pupils' knuckles
if they erred. Years later, when I carried village papers
aging ladies lied they'd find for me
some pieces of his music in their rambling attics.
They cried to me how much they cared for him.
I carry carefully one memory of him,
sharp look under metal rimmed eyes,
but I was just an infant when he died.
Through my youth I wished he had tried to teach me art.

II
Why when I was just a child I pretended to play
on the great open Atlas stretched across my lap
as I listened to the ancient fading radio
in the corner of our parlor.

III
My aunt lifted up my fingers
and placed them one by one on the keyboard, naming notes.
It seemed such a tender thing to me.

IV
But when she wasn't home my fond, clement uncle
let me clatter away, seated at the ancient throne.
Later I convinced the grade school teacher I could play
like fat Junior Odell used to do
when we kids laid our heads down on desks to take our naps,
but it was dreadfully bad when I began to clang
the piano, random and loud.
I was quickly, harshly removed from the spinning stool
and made to stay in after school.

72

V

One day after much long thought I begged a grown-up girl
who was on my paper route
to give me lessons and she coyly agreed but charged
a nickel each. Still I didn't care because I liked
to sit on the brown bench next to her and feel her long girl
fingers guiding my boy ones slowly over the keys.
I began to break into set pieces as if to speak.
I remember in my primer "The Happy Farmer."

VI

In college I paid my good friend Stephen Barrister
who majored in piano and who was fond of boys
fifty cents to give me lessons at 7 a.m.
I was light headed from lack of sleep and the lessons
seemed to make me high and soon I
really loved the piano.
Once I played Debussy's "Submerged Cathedral"
where the mythic sunken Church slowly
emerges from underneath the water louder
and louder until you hear the chimes
like a full-scale chorale.
It's all chords repeated in the same hand positions,
but then I thought to myself,
Gad, "This is really beautiful!"

VII

Having started late I specialized in slow movements—
never developed the agility for speed;
first movement of the "Moonlight Sonata" and second of the
                                                    "Pathetique."
My friend and I climbed into the Carnegie Music
Collection in the basement of Barnes Hall and played Brahms
concertos in the dark middle
of the night, and I broke into the chapel to play
the Baldwin Grand whose beloved, dark black shapely skirt
I undressed slowly on the stage, and I can tell you
these were some of the plain happy days of my brash life.

VIII

Once when I broke in Mary Beth Turacek, the school's
leading scholarship pianist,
was playing Debussy's "Isle of Joy"
and waves of sound broke over me, quite hidden away
in the darkened church. There are great climaxes of tone
and every one of the cells in my skin trembled
like its own little place of joy.

IX

In my senior year at school I remember
my piano teacher Miss Schram
once played for me with swollen arthritic hands
a few thumbs-crossed-over notes of a Schumann Romance,
and I sensed that day I was peculiarly blest.
It was mainly for Miss Schram with whom I fell in love.
I outdid myself in the school's final recital:
Played the slow movement of his
F# Minor Piano Sonata Johannes Brahms
had written at twenty.
It is very rich and reads like an orchestral piece.
I was also only twenty and jealous of him—
no, that's not quite the word, for his music made me feel
I must somehow find a way to change my very life.
It's not an easy piece; even in the andante
there are seven notes on one hand.
Don't ask me how I did it,
but my fulfillment came when my beloved Miss Schram
moved back to the loges
where the recitalists mingled
and said to me, "Jack, that was simply gorgeous!"

Avocado

(for Robert Bly)

It is a green globe like a vegetable light bulb
with a stem to meet either soil or small living tree;
it is mottled like an old man's face or is wizened
like the enormous head of a fetus. Now the stem
has come away from a navel.
It has the stolid heft of a stone. The smell seeps up
and leads the mind far away to the earth's ancient cave.
Its taste is also pungent dirt with a kind of bark
that is quite difficult to chew:
Here is the small tomb of woman.
Mother smells its fresh soil even with her dead sense. She feels
its husk. Her body inside is the soft flesh of fruit,
and her heart this oval green core.
Her grief, her anger is that she
no longer has life, but the stuff of her breathes a residue
that has remained in earth
and in the minds of the children.
Oh, now I know her skin sighs green
as this fluted fruit: her spirit
is the taste of it, transmuted.

A Month of Saints

Well, I am sorry to admit
I missed Mass on August fifteenth,
the Feast of the Virgin's Assumption into heaven.
Her body is here in the world
somewhere, or is that heaven home
outside our own world? In any case
the bodies of Mary and Christ
both are still alive someplace that shall be known to us
at the center of the universe. Mary's body
suffered the anguish of adolescence and the first
menstrual flows that prepared her womb
for the fetus of Jesus planted by the angel's song.
He burgeoned in her and he swam
in her amniotic sea linked by the placenta
that pulsed with her red virgin's blood
and tied his life into woman's life as they still bind
together, man and woman's body somewhere around:
Christ, who lived his young childhood as a carpenter's aid
and underwent puberty like you and me quite complete—
the upset of wet dreams in his fresh celibate life.
Ah, Christ did you not suffer too
even as you began to teach at twelve
pains of the adolescent heart, agonies of self!
The bodies of Christ and Mary hurt and sweat as ours,
and they defecate too like us.
It is a great solace to know
their bodies beautifully changed
are together still, and they shine
on all relationships of men
and women, and the two of them
reflect in the androgynous
life we each of us live out, the man in the woman
and the woman inside the man.
Why we are each of us blest by their permanent lives.

II

And I missed Mass on St. Augustine's Day, the twenty eighth
of August: Augustine, whose lewd father leered at him
naked at his bath and battered
his wife St. Monica, for he was an ignorant
and angry man. The young Augustine always loved to play
and whether "nuts" or "birds" or bouts
of sin he played the game to win.
He showed a literary streak early but hated Greek.
His mother didn't understand all his boyish pain
although she wept and prayed hard that he would come to God.
The child also prayed in school hoping to avoid that beating
which cuts a sensitive aesthete.
Their home was in the northern village of Tagaste where
many Roman roads crossed. The married saint was twenty three
the year she heard Augustine's loud complaint. She gave him
milk, but having learned to tipple
in her father's cellar as a young girl fetching wine
she was afraid of drink, and so for all Augustine's
later sicknesses and chronic fears Monica
only gave him tears. The saint's secret faith,
her creed, and solemn parts of Mass
she loved so well she was not allowed to tell, but when
the boy was young the sacred salt
was placed upon his tongue. It marked a claim upon him
but did not serve his need or solve her pain, and Austin's
pagan dad was little help. Monica told her son
of Christian love and asked the boy
becoming man to use his gifts for this and not for fun.
She spoke with saintly indignation of the evil
ways of fornication and begged him
not to break the laws of Christians.
He smiled at what he thought were simple words of woman.
He took a mistress. Still he never could escape her
prayers no matter where he fled. She dreamed a shining youth
walked toward her standing on a rule.
Augustine went to school where all the students danced

77

the Bacchic rite instead of Mass
and read the ribald book of a
native son, Apuleius' *Golden Ass*. College days
were spent in "Babylon" he later said. He watched the jigs
of courtesans around their fertile gods and saw too
the single-eyed or double-sexed or the missing-mouthed
mosaics preserved along the water front (as bright
as jars in sun) for the tourists' looks.
The Carthaginian shore also bore, too huge to have
a ticket sale, a monster reeking whale, and Austin
thought of that which carried Jonah
underneath the sea on that awful trip that alters
men sometimes and sets them free. A sea
of tears, a great fish of prayers which Monica sent her
son bore him from his Carthaginian house of lust.
He fled from home and went to Italy. The cooling
tides of Christ reached him at Milan where St. Austin's life
and Monica's death began. As one in mystic vision
they watched the formal lights of Christ
above the vast Ostian Sea.
"My dear God," St. Austin said, "Too late have I loved thee!"
and cried hereditary tears when his mother died.

III
Thinking of Mary's body and Austin's pagan youth
I went to Mass on September fifteenth, the Feast Day
of Our Lady of Sorrows, who stood beside the tree
of Christ pierced with the same keen sword.
The Letter to the Hebrews says on this day of Mass,
"In the time when Christ was in the flesh he offered prayers
and supplications with great cries
and tears to God who was able to rescue him from death."
This Feast was a joyous time, for a young woman friend
dressed in a suit of rust and blue
made her first Communion at the age of twenty-two.

I learned in a bar, as we conversed the night before,
she had been baptized as a child
but had never walked to the altar rail for holy bread.
The young woman and three of her friends confessed at Mass
and we all passed to the front of the Church through the nave
with this lovely-eyed brown haired girl,
an artist and so a handmaid of God's creation,
and took the host upon our tongues
and drank the holy blood from the plain brown chalice of wood.
Graced and happy then we all danced off in our small bunch
for a fine Sunday champagne brunch.
The table was top heavy with Sunday specialties—
Eggs Benedict and Florentine and freshly baked bread.
And at the table with us that good day were Austin,
Monica and the radiant, broad
shades of the bright bodies of Mary and Christ our Lord.

Manhattan Movements

My friend Daniela met us in her Subaru
after we had found our way through a crowd or two
at legendary LaGuardia,
and Tim and I went off on a prearranged sojourn
to Mother Cabrini's tomb in Fort Tryon Park—
one hundred and ninetieth street
way out the line on the A train.
We visited her bones in their black habit with wax mask,
her skeleton which for certain will rise up again
for that is what it means to be a saint. We knelt,
and I prayed for my family
and the new found friendship with Tim,
who is Christ's age at thirty-three.
Then we touched each other's fingers
with the holy water and walked off into the park
in the October sun. I felt young
and smiled at the aging faces
of couples sunning themselves on benches on the walks.
I am fifty-eight, but this day
was a respite from my age.
Tim and I stood by the wall and watched the passing ships
like those visions of Fellini
on the gorgeous blue-black Hudson.
We didn't talk much, both of us wrapped up in our thoughts
as we approached The Cloisters, Medieval branch
of the Metropolitan Museum, monastery
carted over stone by stone from Spain
and then reconstructed around a small central court.
It is easy to be overwhelmed here where they store
what is thought to be the true chalice of Jesus Christ,
where the polychromed and gilded
wood Pietà strikes to the heart with its anguished
faces of the pierced Christ and the grieving Virgin and friends,
and where the melancholy white unicorn is penned

in a field of bright flowers bleeding from a neck wound,
its beard and tail both majestically curved, heroic.
And the crazed, craven faces of the hunters, their dogs
yelping and nipping from the threads of the tapestries.
One thanks God for the Gregorian chant which sounds there
so beautifully filling the air of the Cloisters.
Tim and I left, caught the subway,
and descended into the frenetic city again.

II

On the next day, we went to the Light Gallery
to look at the photographs of Harry Callahan.
The naked picture of his wife
Eleanor holding the hand of their small nude daughter
particularly struck me with its beauty. The two
are stepping up onto a sill
fully into the sunlight, the child just visible,
and the wife's thigh and torso are quite handsomely turned.
This photograph is the amazing color of flesh!
And who would believe the ten brilliant red tomatoes
ripening there in another scene on a blue sill?
But this frame has black behind it.
What puts the tomatoes and the nudes both on a sill
but the genius camera eye and hand of Callahan.
And the mannequin—her long forefinger gesturing
beneath her chin! Then in *Venice*
1957 an old man strides in a single
flash of light in a dark chasm
of buildings and blackened canals.
"I wish," writes Callahan, "that more people felt as I:
Photography is an adventure, and the same as life."
We left the gallery and went on to drink champagne
in the loft of the rich boyfriend
of a lovely member of our party. He was gone
to LA and turned the loft over to us for the day.
What a scene: two floors of paintings reached by a spiral
staircase, a greenhouse and an open porch looking out
over lower Manhattan—Wall Street, World Trade Center,
The East River and the Lady—

81

all drenched by sun as the bright edge
of the Brooklyn Bridge whose cables hummed in the afternoon.
There was much pleasant talk, some of it inane,
as we friends sipped champagne and began to reel a bit,
so that some of us flopped onto the twenty-foot couch.
Tim and I went off to dinner
at Daniela's in Brooklyn Heights
where we had stayed the night before.

I remembered the time well because I woke up once
to find I had flung my left arm over his belly
in our sleep, and as he breathed, his diaphragm rose and
fell with the young life he keeps so well.
Tim played on the piano his song "Mannequin's Dream."
Then after fettucine, wine, and good talk, we were off
to listen to the astounding musical statue
and all his gifted friends in Mozart's *Don Giovanni*
our last night in the city.

Staying Awake

We are old, our fields are running wild;
Till Christ again turn wanderer and child—
Robert Lowell

You see I did not want to leave
so I kept the young couple up.
It was the reverse of the scene when Robert Lowell
read at St. John's College the year I turned twenty eight.
I wanted to follow him wherever he would go.
I knew he was headed off to Iowa to teach,
but I had a wife and three kids.
I bathed the kids, put them to bed while she did dishes.
I loved their infantile white flesh and their touseled heads.
I was teaching. I was not free to go, but I held
Lord Weary's Castle in my hand
as I passed from class to class,
and the evening Lowell read I got high on rhyme
and his fierce family vision,
oracles that move through his verse.
I knew he was master then,
and I wanted to apprentice myself under him.
Well, some say that I'm a master now, but on this night
when I was reading Lowell's poems with a pupil
it grew late: I still wanted to take what the student
had to share. I am sixty and am tired of giving.
So I overstayed and kept the couple up, I said,
away from their conjugal bed.

John Logan on the deck of the house boat where he lived in Seattle, April 14, 1966.

Bridges of Faithful Change

PETER MAKUCK

> *What falls away is always. And is near.*
> *I wake to sleep and take my waking slow.*
> *I learn by going where I have go—*
> Theodore Roethke

Essential to John Logan's poetry is the sense of human life as an odyssey through time and space, each poem mapping the internal and external moves of the poet as he pursues epiphany and momentary peace. Logan's first three books (*Cycle for Mother Cabrini, Ghosts of the Heart*, and *Spring of the Thief*) were written at Notre Dame University where he taught between 1951-1963; in a number of ways they bear the impress of that time and place, and establish themes and methods that abide in subsequent work; they are Catholic in preoccupation, touched with pre-*aggiornamento* God-ache and guilt; they contain poems with fine music—assonance and alliteration, slant and internal rhyme. In "Pagan Saturday," an early poem, Logan remembers boyhood when his "limbs and body / Sang," but now he tries to understand the fallen body with its mysteries and sorrows, the relationship of spirit to flesh, of love to sexuality—themes delineated in the title poem of his first book:

> I say this
> For flesh is my failing:
>
> That it shall fall is my
> Salvation. That it shall not
> Conquer is my blind hope.
> That it shall rise again
>
> Commanding, is my fear.
> That it shall rise changed
> Is my faith . . . .

Change is one of Logan's favorite words, carrying often the sense of transformation. Frequent verbs are love, yearn, heal, hope, and feel. Recurring nouns are grace, art, tenderness, resurrection, flesh, peace, God, ghost, home, brother, mother, father, son, sister—all either teachers or guides (two more words frequent in the Logan lexicon) on the learner's odyssey. Though not a narrow believer in word counts, I think that even first-time readers of Logan cannot fail to notice the recurrence of certain words—words which are signposts, indications of concerns, clues to essentials like his abiding preoccupation with the body problematic. In "The Death of Southwell," a paradox of the flesh is again sounded: "But if the healing soul / Slough from it this wanted / Flesh, it will abandon too / These hundred melancholy loves." Healing is sought, but with the simultaneous fear that if realized, the song produced by sorrow will disappear.

Many of the poems in these early books are allusive, heavily epigraphed—sometimes three to the poem—and press the reader with a need for learning: Augustine, Marcel, Pliny, Homer, Virgil, Xenocrates, the Church Fathers, and major figures of Palgrave. But Logan is a poet of more than one mode, and in these same books one finds poems like "The Picnic," an oblique but immediate narrative of sexual discovery not filtered through the prism of learning, allusion, or applied mythology. With the advent of the Eliot-hating '60s and his next book, *The*

John Logan in Ravenna Park, Seattle, April 14, 1966.

Zigzag Walk (1969), the mode of the plain poem gains ascendancy though Logan's love of classical literature and the Joycean method is still apparent.

"Spring of the Thief," from the last book written at Notre Dame, is an important poem in Logan's progress, for it represents a perfect marriage of the two modes as well as a change in attitude toward Catholic orthodoxy, paying as it does more than mere lip service to the doctrine of flesh as Temple of the Holy Spirit. Logan begins by describing a walk around St. Joseph's Lake one Sunday after Mass during Lent. Glimpsing the bronze "Christ and Thieves" atop a nearby hill, he questions the validity of confession if it frees us from guilt only to go out and sin again. A sin of the flesh has caused the speaker more than once to strip and roll in the mud or snow like "St. Francis with his Brother Ass / or a hard bodied Finn . . . ." And, once oblivious, he found himself as if washed up "at some ancient or half-heroic shore" and was

> ashamed that I was naked there.
> Before Nausicaä and the saints. Before myself.
> But who took off my coat? Who put it on?
> Who drove me home?
> *Blessed be sin if it teaches men shame.*
> Yet because of it we cannot talk
> and I am separated from myself.
> So what is all this reveling in snow and rain?
> Or in the summer sun when the heavy gold
> body weeps with joy or grief or love?
> When we speak of God, is it God we speak of?
> Perhaps his winter home
> is in that field where I rolled or ran . . .
> . . . .
> Ekelöf said there is a freshness
> nothing can destroy in us—
> not even we ourselves.
> Perhaps that
> *Freshness* is the changed name of God.
> Where all the monsters also hide
> I bear him in the ocean of my blood
> and in the pulp of my enormous head.
> He lives beneath the unkempt potter's grass
> of my belly and chest.
> I feel his terrible, aged heart
> moving under mine . . . can see the shadows
> of the gorgeous light
> that plays at the edges of his giant eye . . .
> or tell the faint press and hum
> of his eternal pool of sperm . . . .

We see elements of a style that will become familiar. A mixture, for instance, of the sacred and profane. Like the works of D.H. Lawrence and Walt Whitman, Logan's poems will become more frankly erotic, and the eroticism will be both homosexual and heterosexual, if not androgynous. The element of guilt will be present in his later poems as well, but its source will be more secular, will more often be the product of what Logan calls in *The Bridge of Change* any "offense against love" ("Believe It"). Logan will not lose interest in the question of God and transcendence; he simply begins to hear a rumor of angels outside the orthodox church. He finds hints of the divine in art and the struggles of artists, realizing that art is the closest that many people in a largely secular, post-Christian world come to religion, to the awakening of their deepest, richest, most loving feelings. In interviews, often responding to questions about the religious nature of his work, Logan is fond of quoting John Crowe Ransom that poetry is a "secular form of piety . . . miraculism everywhere." He has also said that "poetry and love are the two places where this awareness of a common bond beyond alienation is found" (*A Ballet for the Ear*, p. 47). But his best discussion of poetic process and religious poetry appears in an essay; the last paragraph, so central to Logan's developing poetic, is worth quoting:

> We have the impression that in some way every poem resurrects, giving long life magically to what is gone. Elegies give us again what we don't have and want. We know they are not for the dead. They are consolations for the living. Poems are resurrecting acts, recreative, saving or perhaps damning the members of the poet's own internal, mystical family, the parts and people he finds in himself, some of them really dead, such as the boy he once was or the mother he once had, all of them dead or below the surface in him as relics of himself which he resurrects in his poems, putting them into relations of peace or violence he wants for them, though ultimately . . . the poem itself is a peace, a paradise which delights and in which tensions are resolved and everything is changed into the beautiful and the lasting, into a promised land where the ark docks, where the cycle of time, a destructive thing . . . is telescoped, and visitation, conception, nativity, Good Friday, are simultaneous with each other and issue at once in an Easter . . . . Christian images find their unity not only in the liturgical year and in the life of the Holy Family but also in every event of art.

Although writing about Dylan Thomas, Logan is essentially describing his own view of the religious nature of poetry. The above-quoted essay was published in 1960 (it is reprinted in *A Ballet*) and in the same essay are the seeds of his growing ideas about the holy family of art, about the way "Love, like art, puts two together to make one, building a higher unity." In the same essay: "The artist's ark rescues us too, for a while . . . ." Three years after the publication of this essay, Logan lyrically elaborates the idea that shared artistic experience creates family. Here is a part of "To a Young Poet Who Fled":

> The magic of the mouth that can melt to tears the rock
> of hearts. I mean the wand of tongues that charms the exile
> of listeners into a bond of brothers, breaking
> down the lines of lead that separate a man from a
> man, and the husbands from their wives, in these old, burned
>   glass
> panels of our lives.

Logan, writing in a more recent essay (1971), might as well be glossing his own poem: "The poet is an anonymous lover I believe, and his poetry is an anonymous reaching out, which occasionally becomes personal . . . . At the personal moment a mysterious thing happens, which reminds us of magic, and hence of the power of Orpheus: the loneliness each of us feels locked inside his own skin, and the anonymous reaching each of us does therefore becomes a *bond* and hence we are neither alone nor anonymous in the same sense as we were before." Surely one of the achievements of *The Bridge of Change* and one of the ways it achieves unity is Logan's active interest in the reader, the kind of tender concern one has seen rarely in poets since Whitman (I'm not talking about poets who *assault* the reader—they can be found too easily). In *The Zigzag Walk*, the poet on a number of occasions addresses the reader directly as, for example, in "Three Moves": "I have no priest for now. / Who / will forgive me then. Will you?"

Theologically, Logan has traveled far from the "Spring of the Thief," and one could profitably discuss "Three Moves" in light of the God-is-dead movement or the kind of poetry which makes of the reader a secular priest/confessor (the two not unrelated I think). As in earlier poems, forgiveness is at stake, and the work of the poet is to learn to forgive himself (William Stafford once said, in a context I can no longer resurrect, "We have to learn to forgive ourselves—but not too easily."), and periodically Logan accomplishes the arduous piecework of self-absolution. Occasionally he checks his progress with the reader. Sometimes he actively pursues us as in the last poem of *The Zigzag Walk*, "The Search," where he asks, "But for whom do I look?" and tries to understand why he will spend nights walking the streets, haunting bars, why he will hurt friends and family by leaving them to fly to distant places for the healing warmth of *other* families and friends. Is the search for the "ghost of my youth"? Is it for "The father who will be the mother? / Sister who will be the brother?" He doesn't know and sometimes comes close to panic.

So now the panicked thumbs of my poem pick
through the grill. They poke
the lock
and put out a hand and then an arm.
The limbs of my poems
come within your reach.
Perhaps it is you whom I seek.

Somebody says that to be a person is to be in search of another person,
but the issue is deeper. The "you" of the bottom line is not the an-
swer. If Rilke was, as Logan says, his poet/father, we know that Augus-
tine was another father figure, and the restlessness in this poem has a
familiar ring, except that Logan will not allow himself to rest in an easy
"Thee." The reader/you is only a provisional answer; the search con-
tinues from poem to poem, faithful to Augustine's notion of man as a
mystery to himself and containing within himself intimations of the
divine.

Logan's poetry over the years has managed to shed some of its sexual
guilt. The shame he felt about his nakedness in "Spring of the Thief"
seems gone in later work. In fact, he enjoys his naked flesh and that of
others in "Poem: Tears, Spray, and Steam," last title in the collection
Only The Dreamer Can Change The Dream. The poem, in memory of
Eric Barker, if not quite an elegy, is nonetheless a consolation for the
living, an act of resurrection serio-comic in tone, a buoyant benediction
for the book. The speaker, Eric Barker, and another friend—all hung-
over and in need of healing—invade a grotto-like bath exposed to a
beach in Big Sur where there is an Esalen teacher and "three naked girls
in three corners of the big tub . . . ." They strip, immerse themselves,
float their "masculine flowers," and, as it comes to pass in California,
eventually reach each other. They take turns reading William Butler
Yeats to the girls and to each other, taking care not to wet the book.
Eric Barker is also a singer of bawdy songs ("My long / delayed erec-
tion . . . / rises in the wrong direction.") More people arrive, strip, and
join this motley aquatic family: "Eric Barker takes a leak, / begins recit-
ing Keats, / and we all bathe and sing together / in the new waters of
brother, sister."

*

The Bridge of Change (1981) measures development more than
change, for there are no radical thematic or stylistic departures here
(most noticeable is the longer line, broken strangely at times). What
we witness is the deepening of design, the way weathering wood more
clearly exposes its grain. Though Logan's poems have become less
Catholic, more open and less shamed by matters sexual, they seem to
resist the with-it thinking that would have us shed our "hang-ups" and

not feel guilt or shame about anything. As in the earlier "Three Moves," Logan still believes that, like the "foolish ducks," if we lack a "sense of guilt," there is no "hope of change." In this volume, the sense of guilt often derives from an inability to bridge the distance to others, to change and renew a human relationship gone wrong. "Poem For My Brother" begins *The Bridge of Change*, wherein Logan returns to the family, that familiar first circle of encounter, and the paradise lost of childhood, except that the fraternal relationship described was never quite Edenic. The subject of brothers reaches all the way back to "The Brothers: Two Saltimbanques" (*Ghosts of the Heart*, 1960), though the sunlit innocence and moment of felt grace is gone from this earlier picture of siblings riding the train home from a day at the ballpark. "Poem for My Brother" is a work as powerful as any I know about familial conflict, about resurrecting the past to understand why fraternal relations have become thorny and, as suggested in the Dylan Thomas essay, about the resolution of that tension within a paradise which is the poem. The brothers are simply different—one plays football, the other is in the marching band—but at bottom reflections of each other. Logan tries to bridge these differences. Bridges imply water, and few Logan poems are far from that transforming element:

> once we swam together in
> the Nishnabotna river
> near home, naked, our blue overalls piled together
> by the water, their copper
> buttons like the bronze glints in my ring. I remember
> once when I was very young
> I looked deep into a pool
> of blue water—we had no mirror—and I was so
> amazed I looked over my shoulder, for I did not
> imagine it was me, caught
> in that cerulean sky.
> Thinking it was someone other, I tell you I con-
> fused myself with my brother!

Logan's sometimes awkward and unfortunate enjambments seem produced by syllabics settled on in advance (in this case 8 and 13 are the usual numbers), but the penultimate line quoted is wonderfully functional, underscoring the theme of reconciliation by calling attention to the dual possibilities of "con-fused," reminding us also of the estranged double of a brother we have previously seen in poems like "Lines for Michael in the Picture." But here the yearning for reunion is more pronounced; the speaker thinks about how he no longer communicates with his brother and how their children, cousins, don't even know each other. He looks at the ring he has just bought and says

So, I would have you know I
want this ring to *engage* us
in reconciliation.
Blue is the color of the heart.
I won't live forever. Is it too late now to be
a brother to my brother?
Let the golden snake bend round
again to touch itself and
all at once burst into azure!

Whatever else happens here, there is a resolution of tensions, the kind of self-absolution we have seen before. In my discussions of these lines with students, I find they usually and *realistically* hope that it is not "too late" for a brother to be a brother. The sentiment is right, but we have to consider carefully the last three lines, and remember Auden's comment about poetry making nothing happen.

In "Grace," reconciliation occurs—perhaps only *in* the poem. The speaker holds an artist's sculpted box that is strung with musical wires, threaded bits of garnet; in candle light, he sees his childhood loom up and moans "with all the old, sure pleasure / of what I'd thought I'd lost come back again." The speaker pictures himself and his brother splashing, cavorting in deep-image water that irrigates much of Logan's poetry, reminding one of Melville and Bachelard, *L'eau et les rêves*. The poem concludes in a prelapsarian dream:

my brother and I, unborn twins who lie entangled
in each other's developing
limbs. Soon we will be born! He and I will taste of milk
for the very first time! And taste of strawberry pop
and of bright bananas. And we will eat, my brother
and I, a great, shining, autumn-red apple fallen
from our father's tree as if from the long sky, and *you*
too will taste this apple with us
for we all have the same mother, and her name is Grace.

The italicized *you* is, of course, the same who appears toward the end of "Poem For My Brother": the anonymous reader/lover who also participates as secret sharer in this great archetypal story.

In "Returning Home," and subsequent sections of the book, Logan tries to fix the location of "home." Is there a home at the end of the odyssey? Or does the odyssey end? The search takes the speaker to the homes of his sons and their families where he basks and heals for a time in the warmth of their presence. But each poem, however humorous in tone or affirmative in its images, ends with a realization of the limits of love and the speaker's sense of himself as the finite odd man out.

"A Day in the Sun" describes a proud father with a son who is learning photography, an art form that has long interested Logan and constitutes another thematic thread in the design. Together they elaborately compose a few frames of themselves backgrounded by eucalyptus and flowering iceplant and set the camera on delay. But something has gone wrong; "None of the photos will come out." They laugh, but a day in the sun has been shadowed: "We turn toward the car, / our thoughts a bit reflective, far." As in "Five Preludes For Buffalo's Own Forest Lawn," the image and experience of father and son is not really lost because of the "one who makes now this protective poem." And the poem in its own way is superior to the photos because the images are not reductive, do not tyrannize—vivid tone and voice not lost as in a photo.

"Coming of Age" begins with the father riding in his son David's "blue turquoise brand new truck" on the way to Buck's Lake for a picnic, the younger boys, Stephen and Paul, in the back with a girl friend. At the lake, they strip and "Suddenly David dives, streaks from a high, jutting rock: / a wild swan just turned twenty-one." The Yeatsian beauty combines with an awareness and acceptance of finality, for the children swim to the other side, leaving him alone with chilly thoughts. As they move toward him again he says:

> I leave my
> reveries in the breeze-blown foam,
> which wafts to the manzanita and the golden oak.
> Their new lives shape in this, my wake.

What is implied in the last word of the poem is dealt with more directly in "Returning Home," a prose poem where the poet arrives in his hometown, finding the old house gone, and gone, one after another, the familiar landmarks, even the "stam pipe" or watertower. At the cemetery (in *Ghosts of the Heart*, Logan describes another such trip in "On The Death of The Poet's Mother Thirty-Three Years Later"), he finds that the "plot is thick, is full." The land has "sprouted much more pine and spruce: it has put on population in the fifty years since I was born." The grave he imagined for himself has already been filled with other family members and there will be no place for him beside his mother's "changing body." Thomas Wolfe has told us we can't go home again, and Logan discovers that the "brick house where once I went to school is gone . . . . My home room is gone! Now it's a storage bin for grain." Logan dramatizes, as James Dickey does in "Looking for the Buckhead Boys," the impossibility of going home except through memory and imagination, except through the process of poetry. When at the end of the earlier poem about visiting his mother's grave, Logan wrote, "So here my mother lies," he was describing the poem both as grave and home. Similarly, at the end of "The Bridge of Change," having learned that home is both a state of mind and a place created by language, he acts as a guide, leading us to a Paris street, real yet beautifully suggestive, "our street, *Rue Gît le Coeur, Here Lies the Heart*."

This side of the grave, however, the heart yet yearns for love and for the lost Edenic home of childhood. Logan marries both these themes to the idea of poetry as compensation in the extraordinary "Assateague," a poem of place written in tight syllabic quatrains but with casual, nicely slanted rhymes. Assateague is a marshy island where dwarf ponies came ashore from wrecked Spanish galleons and still survive on the wild inaccessible beaches, but are once a year rounded up, driven inland

> and for the rest of their bound
> lives they yearn for salt and sedge
> they fed on under the ridge
> of snow along the island edge
>
> as we yearn for our childhood
> or the love we never had
> or else had but could not keep
> until we came to Assateague.

As in Part V of "Poem in Progress," Logan is walking with two young people who are in love, seeming to long for the same kind of love relationship they have. In his *Confessions of a Knife*, the poet/surgeon Richard Selzer writes, "A man and a woman love themselves in each other; together, they become a home." It is this kind of a home that Logan misses, yearns for, and thinks of in connection with the young couple. The ponies who are driven inland, but remember their home, function as a metaphor for that backward yearning.

*

Search, love, art, travel, fathers and sons, water and bridges—these are some of the themes and images that knit the central section, "Poem in Progress," to the rest of the book and create a complex unity. Though Logan's bridges from poem to poem are firmly and successfully established, his performance in individual poems is uneven. The series returns to Logan's earlier mode, and we find a host of classical deities used to underpin an eight-part narrative about fathers and sons, about the growth of friendship between two men whose ages could make them father and son. In the first poem, cast as a dream, the speaker/son drifts in a ship down main streets through "land-locked midwestern towns" until he sees some old men who remind him of his father. He says he still loves his dead absent father, yearns for his advice, and laments the talk that never transpired between them. But there is some residual anger and the resurrected portrait of this inarticulate, uncomprehending father has changed little since *Ghosts of the Heart* where, in

94

"Lines to His Son On Reaching Adolescence," he says, "My father never taught me anything . . . ." And in "Returning Home," he recalls listening to radio opera on Saturday afternoon while his father listened to games in a downtown bar and came "home at six o'clock fuming. Is that damn thing still going?" In "First Prelude," the tension between father and son is unresolved, and the father is not quite absolved by a son who still relives the frustrated communication which made him angry with himself: "Instead I ran my buddy's car ninety miles an hour / down Highway 48 outside of town and jacked off / when I got home." The problem with the poem is that it careens like the car, veers, is blurred. The lines too are sometimes ungainly, lines maddeningly broken: "I can hear them as the ageless, orange moon ri- / ses over the small hill or houses." Ri-ses?

In the second poem, "Second Prelude. Reality in Albuquerque: The Son," the speaker is himself the absent, delinquent father submitting to a tragi-comic interrogation by a bartender's truant son, a "bright-eyed Chicano kid."

> He asks me where all my kids are.
> "In New York where I live," I lie.
> Then tell the truth, that I am flying back there tonight.
> "And your wife?" Third degree, I think. Well, part of bar talk.
> "Why, New York too," I lie again.
> How the hell can I tell this kid
> I hardly ever see my sons
> because they are three thousand miles
> away from me (and then some). Perhaps *you* understand
> what I mean—but him? Both of us
> in the bar at ten A.M. He walks to the juke box
> with a quarter given by his father, then looks back,
> admits he cannot read well. So
> we select together, and agree on two pieces,
> playing first that morning song, "Bridge Over Troubled Water."

Most bars are backed with mirrors, but the situation itself is here the mirror, presenting funhouse reflections that are at the same time alarming, and poignant, especially in light of other poems where Logan has written so powerfully about that most awesome of responsibilities—being a parent. One thinks, for example, of "Lines to His Son on Reaching Adolescence," the closure in particular: ". . . from now on I will not plead / As I have always done, for sons / Against their fathers who have wronged them. / I plead instead for us / Against the sons we hoped we would not hurt."

"Second Prelude" is perhaps the most successful *and* independent part of "Poem in Progress." The fifth section, "Interlude. The Colombian Statue: Archetype," can also stand independently and is important for the way it pursues the themes of childhood, friendship, art, and the anonymous lover. We are reminded of "Assateague," for the speaker is again with two young people in love and they show him "their childhood river" where they swam naked as kids. Because his poems have meant so much to Kathy and Jay, they give him their most treasured possession, a carved wooden statue of a man from Colombia:

(I remembered at once the story Neruda tells
of the source in his early life for his sense of what poetry
is: an exchange between strangers—
the boy he had never seen beyond the garden wall
who had left a toy white lamb in a niche, and the child
Neruda took it leaving his prize pine cone instead,
and the anonymous boy clutched it quick for himself.)

The poems just mentioned have unity, clarity, and clean movement. The others are less focused and are busy. "Plato In Florida," for example, brings the young friend into the narrative, and with him come Socrates, Alcibiades, Aristophanes, Artemis, Proteus (for the major theme), Phaedrus, Aphrodite, Diana, Tiresias, Zeus, Leonard Bernstein, and, well, the androgynous David Bowie (androgyny will be an important theme in "Traveling," the last section of the book). The friendship that develops at a picnic in the pastoral Florida sun and later on the cold beach at New Smyrna is celebrated still later in "First Reunion in New Orleans: The Father as King of Revels." Here, the city allows Logan to allude to the important friendship between elder Sherwood Anderson and young William Faulkner, and the Mardi Gras setting provides an opportunity to introduce a thematic figure like Proteus, thus marrying the mythological and the contemporary in a way that is less awkward. However, in the last section, "Second Reunion in San Francisco: The Lost Son," something has gone wrong. The Cliff House where speaker and friend have their reunion drink "has burnt and been built and burnt and built three times," simultaneously suggesting change, chance, and fragility, the kind of fragility that is revealed with great power by a terrible incident near the end of the poem. But first, the speaker/guide begins to make some associative leaps from the nearby Sutro Baths (now burnt) he has seen in photos to Diana's Baths in the Melos Valley of Greece, then back to turn-of-the-century San Francisco, the death of coolies, the guilt of a wealthy man, then back to ancient history, Athene, and the Smyrna colonists who were from Lesbos. Finally, as if sensing his own tedium and the limits of his audience, he says: ". . . but let's both just fuck all this and have our drink." Funny and shrewdly proleptic, but the problems remain.

In "The Bridge of Change," Logan's knowledge of Paris history works to great advantage and makes the past *live* in our imaginations as few other poets could. But here we have a kind of floating, historical *connaissance de luxe* that threatens to distract from what is truly powerful—the fall of a young boy from the rough rocks into the treacherous surf. It takes the friends a moment to realize, what with the topless show in the bar, that they "are seeing a boy drown!" The speaker runs for the phone. Soon the police and firemen arrive and futilely attempt to rescue the boy. Watching them, the speaker measures his distance from the midwest childhood and pastoral innocence of Florida described in an earlier poem:

> There are no Florida peacocks here, odd as they are,
> no iridescent Iowa
> pheasants. Giddy seagulls jabber around, and the sand-
> pipers pick their way. Well, we are all voyeurs, vultures
> round the boy who cannot be found,
> death rising cold in his groin from the thrust of the sea
> that once gave all of us our birth.

The scene itself and Logan's literal orchestration are masterful, putting us in mind of something Bergman or Fellini might film. When the Coast Guard helicopter whirrs above this scene that is "sunset-lit," the aircraft described as a "spider-like parody of God," I think of the final moments in *Through A Glass Darkly*. Logan, unfortunately, is not satisfied with the helicopter image itself, and he strains for the applied mythology: "jealous Minerva, / useless *deus ex machina*." Feeling lucky that it was not his friend, Michael, who slipped from the cliff, Logan, relieved but sad, concludes this section of the book by reminding both Michael and us that the ship of this eight-part narrative is no *bateau ivre*; the poet is still quite capable of sound navigation:

> Perhaps it is
> your life—or *yours*, or *yours*, or *yours*, or *yours*—I felt up-
> stairs in those luminous and dark, hidden levels of
> my own, still quite navigable ship!

*

The last section of the book ("Traveling") gives us again Logan's sense of odyssey, search, as well as an image of man similar to the one captured so beautifully in the title of Julian Green's novel, *Le voyageur sur la terre*. All but one are pilgrimage poems which deal with Yeats, Joyce, Thomas, Hopkins, Hemingway, and bow to the animating and transforming spirit of great works of European art. The poem from which the volume takes its title, "The Bridge of Change," an extraordinary historical meditation in eight parts, has its genesis on The Bridge of Change overlooking L'Ile de la Cité, a place—like the human self—of much beauty and terror. The poem gives us a wonderfully telescoped story of the beginnings and development of Paris on that boat-shaped island in the Seine. At the outset, we notice the island, boat, and water motifs that were present in earlier sections of the book. The first lines present us with a sketch of boys sailing model boats: "The children play at the Luxembourg fountain. / Their small ships catch the wind and sail out and come round again." The technique is almost cinematic; one imagines a *son et lumière* with a series of dramatic historical slides punctuated by the image of a waterclock sailboat swinging again and again close to shore, the boy being a periodic reminder of the poem's epigraph from Rilke: "The bridge barely curved that connects / the terrible with the tender." Throughout the eight parts, Logan juxtaposes past and present, images of darkness and light, great art and ephemeral street performances, bloodshed and beauty. Toward the end of the poem, still thinking perhaps of the early victims of the headsman ("Monsieur de Paris") and of those 2,600 who benefited from the progress of science (the guillotine), Logan returns to one of his old themes, the flesh, as he contemplates the

> jewel of Sainte Chapelle,
> its windows of rose and blue, gold, green, yellow, purple,
> rising fifty feet:
> its spire piercing the foliate,
> layered, many-colored egg of the vault of heaven,
> showering all the primal hues and shadows given—
> bright as the truth reflected in a drop of fresh blood
> or the colors of the body's inner organs hid-
> den before the sure explosion of light that hits them
> at the moment of violent death. — This is a time
> like that of the sun that once a year, just at the dawn
> of winter solstice, lights up an ancient Celtic stone
> grave striking the bones spread on shelves
> with all the colors of the flesh.

In *Ghosts of the Heart*, Logan was already interested in the multiple lives possible for the self and chose an epigraph from Joyce: "We walk through ourselves meeting robbers, ghosts, giants, old men, young men, wives, widows, brothers-in-love. But always meeting ourselves." Most of that list we have seen in earlier poems, but in "Dublin Suite: Homage to James Joyce," we find Logan adding to the inhabitants of the heart by rapturously dreaming over illuminations in the Book of Kells where he sees emblazoned "bent bodies / of fabulous, elongated beasts / linked and feeding beautifully upon each other, / or upon themselves." After wonderfully detailed and cadenced descriptions of the rare, intricate illuminations of devils and angels conjured by "the bold minds of monks," Logan concludes the "Library" section by turning to the reader:

> Ah, friend, look how this Book of Kells
> pictures all our heavens, all our hells.

Since these are pictures of the self, we are not far from the Yeatsian view that, innocence recovered, the soul learns it is "self-delighting, / self-appeasing, self-affrighting."

The last section of the poem is set at Martello Tower and begins with the speaker's observation of "awkward, naked boys" hollering and diving into "the forty-foot hole" where, since Joyce's time, only men have swum, "though now some militant has scrawled / in chalk at the entrance to the spot a woman's sign: / The Venus Mirror." Things have changed even in Dublin. Finally. But Joyce long ago perceived the painful position of women in Irish society, made apparent in his understanding of Molly Bloom and the longing of suppressed women in general. After reading *Ulysses*, Jung wrote to Joyce acknowledging the latter's greater understanding of women. Quoting from that letter, Logan returns to a theme he has sounded previously, namely that the poet as representative man must contain multitudes, must adopt whatever identity will build the bridge from one islanded self to another. Androgyny is sometimes involved. Joyce is, for Logan, a great reminder of human flexibility and potential:

> . . . Joyce, I feel I wear your vest—
> and like you am more than human.
> I too have within myself the boy, man and woman.
> But your clothes make my heart inflate,
> for that is not 'more than human.'
> Why, Diana had the hunter who desired her
> transformed into a deer, his flesh rent by his own dogs.
> How often has the woman punished the man in her?
> Or the man the woman in him?

The poem closes with affirmation and the hope of change.

"Papa's House, Son's Room," one of the best of the pilgrimage poems, picks up some of Logan's more persistent themes: the sins of the fathers, the risk and sometimes terrible price of art, and the teacher/ poet as impossible surrogate father. Though Logan does not say it, the proximity of the poem to the "Dublin Suite" actively suggests that Hemingway's tragedy was that, unlike Joyce, he lacked the sympathy for the woman *and* the boy within himself and never made bridges to these other selves. He did cross daily a literal bridge on his way to write, but it was not a bridge of change and he was neither transformed nor dignified by his art. The patient catalogue of Papa's things, "pictures of *him* / and *his* friends, and souvenirs from all over the world," indicates that Logan is thinking not primarily about public success and failure which so absorbed Hemingway. The theme is personal failure. What haunts the Key West house is not so much the presence of the great writer but the absence of children who lived there too. After a description of Papa's kingly bedroom, Logan asks, "How did those young brothers feel in their plain room beside?" A devastating question.

Finally we learn Logan was Gregory Hemingway's teacher, and they would have coffee after Mass. The boy was quiet and restless and left college before the end of the term: "He never spoke of his father / and, unlike his brother, did not become a hunter." Again we return to the theme of opposed brothers with which *The Bridge of Change* began. From the boy's room overflowing with Papa's things, Logan ponders the Lenten tree about to bloom—a closure which is cautionary in its implications and sends us back to the beginning of the poem to see how, and at what cost, Papa planted his garden and built his fabulous house:

> In Key West, poinciana trees bloom flamboyant red
> before the leaves begin, and here in Hemingway's yard
> the bare Lenten tree soon will bloom
> bright as the blood from Papa's head,
> red as the bricks from the wall he built around the house—
> carting them home from the torn trolley track on Duvall
> Street. Red as the blast from the safe
> after his death—where his wife found the undone ms.
> of *Islands in the Stream*: the father, his friends and sons:
> their unfinished relationships.

Bridges. Islands in the stream. So much of Logan's work is about bridging, change, and transformation. Though the penultimate poem of the book, "Traveling," takes us to those cities of great Italian art, Rome, Venice and Florence, has two literal bridges (The Bridge of Sighs and the Ponte Vecchio), and the theme of healing through beauty, the last poem of *The Bridge of Change* more successfully gathers a number of Logan's major concerns, provides a good conclusion to the book, and this discussion as well. The dedication of "Believe It" tells us that the poem is for Tina Logan, the poet's daughter, and was written after "visiting the Believe It or Not Museum with her in San Francisco." In case we have dismissed as unreal the devils and gargoyles in The Book of Kells and at Notre Dame, we are again asked to look at grotesques like the "two-headed goat," the "sad lamb with seven legs," and the double eyed man "who seemed to watch in me my doubts about my spirit. / Will it snag upon this aging flesh?" This question, of course, is the worry of old, a theme sounded in "Cycle For Mother Cabrini." But the Ripley grotesques induce a sense of unease and guilt as Logan internalizes them. Like the man of Lahore who collected, wrapped, and dragged after him hundreds of pounds of chains, Logan imagines that each "link or each lump in me is an offense against love." Finally, ever interested in the reader, Logan has us partake of tentative conclusions about home and the odyssey:

> I want my own lit candle lamp buried in my skull
> like the Lighthouse Man of Chungking,
> who could lead the travelers home.
> Well, I am still a traveler and I don't know where
> I live. If my home is here, inside my breast,
> light it up! And I will invite you in as my first guest.

So petitioning and inviting us in to see the ghosts of the heart, Logan admits he needs us and, after such transforming poems and lovely bridges, we ought to admit that we need him.

Poetry as Transformation: John Logan's Ghost Dance

ANTHONY PETROSKY

For John Logan, "what makes something poetry in the first place is its musical quarrel with the self, its lyricism,"[1] and although it may appear that Logan's poetry "has undergone many changes since the explicitly Catholic poetry of his first volume, *Cycle for Mother Cabrini,*"[2] there are, I think, enduring themes in his work that have not changed, but have grown into an extraordinarily beautiful body of poetry transforming Logan's quarrels with himself into a continually enlarging brotherhood or community of love and grace.

What are these quarrels with himself, what do they represent, and where do they have their origins? The clearest answers to these questions come from close readings of Logan's poems with attention to the metaphors he creates to represent his relationships with others and himself. Some of the more obvious metaphors he develops reveal themselves in titles of his books. For instance, Mother Cabrini represents a dogged saintliness Logan admires, a persistence in helping others that emanates from a love of mankind. In *Spring of the Thief*, the thief, the crooked angel hanging on the cross next to Christ, becomes a metaphor for redemption—thieves, those who steal from others, are saved by God's absolution, His forgiveness, emanating from love. *The Zigzag Walk*, Logan's fourth book, portrays the search for the self, the universal drive for identity, as a zigzag walk veering here and then there. Searching for identity, for the self that is composed of many selves, is the subject again in *The Anonymous Lover*, and the narrator, the unknown or unidentifiable lover, creates his self-identity in the stories he tells about his personal relationships that, in turn, tell him who he is. In *The Bridge of Change*, Logan develops the metaphor of the bridge, the psychological bridge, the human bridge—love, that connects the terrible with the tender.

These metaphors, as interesting as they are for their repeated connections to love and tenderness, share something else. Underlying them all, giving birth to them, is a larger metaphor having to do with Logan's dramatization of balance and juxtaposition as the source of poetry and lyricism. It is this balancing of polar influences like tender and terrible, love of fulfillment and love of lack (see BC, 38), and male and female (see V, 19) that is responsible for these quarrels or tensions within himself that he refers to as the source of poetry. He dwells on them, articulates them, and tries to reconcile them through love or through some understanding of how they are connected to each other. When the forces or drives of the self (the ego, id, super ego and the compulsion to repeat successful behaviors) attempt to reach some kind of equilibrium or balance after being in a state of conflict with each other or with reality, they create solutions that are, to different degrees, cathartic.[3] Writing and reading are cathartic, for example, because they are open to projections of the self. We project our selves, our quarrels or tensions (and our joys) into what we write and read; and for Logan, these projections have, at their heart, a metaphor of balancing and bridging.

These quarrels with the self, then, emanate from Logan's way of seeing, and being in human relationships. He identifies opposing drives and needs, balances or bridges them through love and understanding, and in this way creates a self-identity through the stories he tells of who he is. His poems articulate these quarrels, these tensions, these tyrannies of the self at an even more primitive level though. For Logan, the male lyric poet

> builds in his work the body of his mother . . . he wishes to give birth to her as she has done for him. In building the body of the parent of the opposite sex through his work the poet establishes a sexual relationship with his own work and dramatizes at the lyric level (the battle with himself, that is) the tragic battle (the battle with the parent). Thus he plays out within himself the primal scene, one part of himself taking the feminine role another the masculine. (V, 19)

This primal (birthing) scene, as Logan calls it, metaphorically represents the process of writing, of giving birth to his poetry; and both its terrible and tender aspects are highlighted, intensified, because of his preoccupations with sins (in the Catholic sense of them). This primal scene, this giving birth to poems, to art, by juxtaposing, balancing, and connecting polar influences, opposites, is part and parcel of Logan's quarrels with the self. It is compounded by the fact that his mother died shortly after his birth, and he is, therefore (at least he tells himself in his poems), a thief in need of his father's forgiveness. He is also, in a sense, exiled from both parents and, consequently, on his own as both mother and father to himself to establish his self-identity.

Logan's search for his father's forgiveness takes him beyond the realm of poetry as secular religion in which language ties people together into a sacred realm, a community where the poet's voice, like the priest's or shaman's,[4] changes fears into a love of mankind capable of warding off anxieties and replacing them with solace. "According to one ethical view" cited by Freud, which, like Logan's, connects religion to the pleasure principle, this readiness for a universal love of mankind and the world represents the highest standpoint which man can reach . . .[5]

But, as Freud goes on to point out, there are two serious problems with this "view," "this readiness for a universal love of mankind." First,

A love that does not discriminate seems to . . . forfeit a part of its own value, by doing an injustice to its object; and secondly, not all men are worthy of love.[6]

When Logan transforms fears and anxieties into solace and love through poetry, he creates a ritualistic solution to his quarrels that resembles an ancient ghost dance where "In unbearable crisis situations, religious prophets are cultural innovators who are able to contrive new social forms and new symbolism to keep all men in society from going individually insane."[7] In a sense, Logan, through poetry, becomes a prophet who contrives the forms and symbols of a brotherhood called together by his prayer, his song in the name of love. While Logan does charm "the exile / of listeners into a bond of brothers" (ST, 11), and while he thusly fights off despair, he also runs the risks pointed out above in Freud's comments on a universal love of mankind. He leaves himself open to being caught in a love that is not discriminating and to being forced to believe that all men are worthy of love.

Logan's ghost dance, then, his poetic ritual where "fear has been transformed into love,"[8] emanates from his relationships with others and himself that dramatize "at the lyric level (the battle within himself, that is) the tragic battle (the battle with the parent)" (V, 19). The quarrels within himself over sin and his mother's death, for example, represent or mirror the larger, primal process of giving birth (to self-identity and poems) by being both mother and father, tender and terrible. His lyricism bridges polar influences like grief and joy, anguish and pleasure through his extraordinary sense of language and its sounds, so his quarrels resonate and travel a zig zag walk to the heart.

In *Cycle for Mother Cabrini*, Logan's quarrel is with the needs of his flesh:

I thank God Mother Cabrini's
Body is subject to laws
Of decay. To me it is
A disservice when flesh

Will not fall from bones
As God for His glory
Sometimes allows. I speak thus
For flesh is my failing:

That it shall fall is my
Salvation. That it shall not
Conquer is my blind hope.
That it shall rise again

Commanding, is my fear.
That it shall rise changed
Is my faith . . .   (CMC, 3)

As a Catholic, he believes sin has its roots in the flesh, in the human
needs that brought about the fall, and he is bewildered, as he says in
"Monologue for the Good Friday Christ," by what he should do:

But Christ what do we do
That hate pain and can't
Pray and are not able
Not to sin . . .   (CMC, 27)

This quarrel, this painful tension within a self that cannot pray and yet
cannot avoid sin is a continual source of grief and torment in Logan's
poetry. In "Poem for My Friend Peter at Pihana" from a much later
book, *The Anonymous Lover*, Logan speaks again about irresolvable
pain:

You are patient with the pain
I keep
          which I can
neither explain
                    (even to myself)
nor escape. And therefore I half
begin
          to love you . . .   (AL, 58)

In "A Trip to Four or Five Towns" from *Ghosts of the Heart* (his sec-
ond volume), he metaphorically sets this same tension in an elegant
lyricism in a seminary in "bellychilling, shoe soaking, factory- /dug-up-
hill smothering Pittsburgh weather" (GH, 75):

A small, slippered priest
pads up. Whom do you seek, my son?
Father, I've come in out of the rain.
I seek refuge from the elemental tears,
for my heavy, earthen body runs to grief
and I am apt to drown
in this small and underhanded rain
that drops its dross so delicately
on the hairs of the flowers, my father,

105

and follows down the veins of leaves
weeping quiet in the wood.

My yellow cab never came,
but I did not confess
beneath the painted Jesus Christ. I left
and never saved myself at all
that night in that late, winter rain.   (GH, 75)

In *Ghosts of the Heart*, Logan begins to consciously wrestle with this tension and locates it in his need for and isolation from adult love and within his own sense of helplessness to control either his desires or dreams:

Our wants are what we are
And what we are is not
The man we hoped, it seems, so what
The hell good are our dreams?   (GH, 39)

A number of the poems in this volume ("Concert Scene" and "Shore Scene" especially) give the sense that although Logan craves the companionship and love of the people he's with, they leave him distant, alienated, and perhaps, they are not what he hoped they would be. Two of the major scenes, a concert where "The hostess brings a tray / Of sherry and a jar of caviar / In ice . . ." (GH, 45) and a beach outing where Logan frees a tricked child "moaning from a low mound of sand, / Abandoned by his friend . . ." (GH, 52), lack the play of polar influences against each other, the tug and pull of desires against their controls, and, finally, they seem too easy and boring. The first three poems in *Ghosts of the Heart*, on the other hand, introduce a tension that carries over and emerges clearly in *Spring of the Thief*. These first three poems speak about mothers, including Logan's who died shortly after his birth. The first, "The Lives of the Poet," paints a picture of a mother who tames the poet by domesticating him, by keeping him from "his life / Of rigorous debauch" (GH, 7); the second, "A Century Piece for Poor Heine," portrays Heine's mother as a domineering monster; and the third, "On the Death of the Poet's Mother Thirty-Three Years Later," tells us "My mother died because / I lived or so / I always chose to believe" (GH, 14). Later on in the third poem, in the last stanza, after Logan tells us he was grown before he found his mother's grave, he says:

So here my mother lies. I do not
Resurrect again her restless
Ghost out of my grievous memory:
She waits the quiet hunt of saints.
Or the ignorance of citizens of hell.

> *And here is laid her orphan child with his*
> *Imperfect poems and ardors, slim as sparklers.*   (GH, 18)

These lines leave the impression that although his mother's death a month after his birth *could be* a terrible legacy, it is not, and the gist of these three poems taken together seems to be an attempt to define the ways of bad and good mothers. In "A Trip to Four or Five Towns," Logan gives a glimpse of mothering ways that please him:

> My friend has a red-headed mother
> capable of love in any kind
> of weather. I am not sure
> what she passes to her daughters
> but from her brown eye and from her breast
> she passes wit and spunk to her big sons.
> And she is small and pleased when they put
> their arms around her, having caught her.   (GH, 77)

The close relationship between this mother and her sons pleases Logan, and we are left with the impression at the end of this book that the brief mention of his mother's death at the beginning of the volume is not exceptionally painful for him.

By the time Logan is writing the poems in *Spring of the Thief*, he has begun to speak openly about his mother's death and the influence it bears on his life. The first section of the first poem in the volume, "Monologues of the Son of Saul," addresses his mother's death in an oblique way through an old story:

> Ah so, our first load of honey heavy Christmas trees.
> Then the sweet Christ comes again. See, in the high truck bed
> the greens spring easy as the thighs of young lovers
> while the aromatic golden gum, gift of The Magus,
> oozes under the light cover of snow, rising slow
> as the milk of the dead. Mothers will survive these rites
> of birth, it is said. We prove it by our liturgy.
> But I do not believe my own theory, and am cursed
> to figure how I was blest at the root of my heart
> by a man sitting underneath a flowering tree
> in a white shirt open at the throat, dark face lucid,
> saying the stories of a father for me. Yet I,
> I have thieved my father's treasure. And I cannot pay.
> On my naked birthday I brought to bed this amber haired,
> shy eyed wife, her face birch white against the linen
> loaf or coif of her pillow. Now, Advent, her quilted,
> copper coffin glows again with a green, harlot's light
> inside my head. Oh I've tried boyishly before to-
> day to lay her virgin ghost in this enormous house,

but still I feel her black teeth click and push at the roots
of its dying blood (or apple) colored bush.   (ST, 3)

Logan chooses to associate his mother's death with his birth, and when
he writes here "I have thieved my father's treasure," he gives Jonathan,
the speaker in this myth, a story that could represent Logan's: in his
birth he thieved his father's wife. What is the price he cannot pay? In
the second section of the poem, Jonathan, knowing the price is his life,
is spared by the Lord God who "sent leaping from the heart of a bush
a saving ram" (ST, 4). In "Lines on His Birthday" from the third sec-
tion of the book, Logan more directly meditates on his birth:

I was born on a street named Joy
of which I remember nothing,
but since I was a boy
I've looked for its lost turning.
Still I seem to hear my mother's cry
echo in the street of joy.
She was sick as Ruth for home
when I was born. My birth
took away my father's wife
and left me half
my life. Christ will my remorse
be less when my father's dead?
Or more. As Lincoln's minister of war
kept the body of his infant boy
in a silver coffin on his desk,
so I keep
in a small heirloom box of teak
the picture of my living father.
Or perhaps it is an image of myself
dead in this box she held?
I know her milk like ivory blood
still runs in my thick veins
and leaves in me an almost
lickerish taste for ghosts:
my mother's wan face,
full brown hair, the mammoth breast
death cuts off at the bone—
to which she draws her bow
again, brazen Amazon,
and aiming deadly as a saint
shoots her barb
of guilt into my game heart.   (ST, 32-33)

This poem strikes similar chords as those played in the first section of
"Monologues of the Son of Saul" and quite different ones than those

presented in "On the Death of the Poet's Mother Thirty-Three Years Later" in *Ghosts of the Heart*. These two laments from *Spring of the Thief* resurrect his mother's ghost, her image, and in the process, locate one of the strongest tensions in Logan's poetry in his mother's death, but it is even more complicated because he also raises the question of forgiveness. Who will forgive him? Will his remorse be less when his father is dead? Is there a way to obtain forgiveness without his father's death? Having the absolution from guilt linked to his father's death must be a frightening thought even though it is not really an absolution but is, rather, a solution that can only lead to more grief. Other than absolution through his father's death, the only other ways forgiveness can come are either directly from the father or from not assuming the guilt to begin with. Logan assumes the guilt, built, as it is, on his mother's death, and his search for his father's forgiveness ensues, and the search gives birth to John Logan's ghost dance, to his ritualistic healing in the name of love through his voice that charms listeners into brotherhoods in this somewhat sacred solution to a human problem.

According to the anthropologist Weston La Barre, ghost dances come about when there is "a cultural breakdown under stress away from technical, secular adaptation into the mystical, fantasied solutions of the sacred cult."[9] One of the examples of a ghost dance La Barre cites involves the Paiute shaman Wovoka who attempted to ritualistically resolve his tribe's increasing anxiety over the white men whom they fought in their losing battle for survival.

> While still a young man, Wovoka became sick with fever in 1899. At this time "the sun died" in a total eclipse, and in a delirium or trance Wovoka was taken to see God. All the people who had died long ago were there in heaven, busy with their games and occupations, happy and forever young. God told him to preach goodness to his people and to practice war no more. They should dance a ceremony that God taught him, to hasten the reunion with the dead . . . Finally he got five songs by which he controlled the weather, one each for mists, snow, showers, storms, and clear weather . . . Jesus, he told the Arapaho and Cheyenne, was now back on earth. They should not fear the earthquake of the new world when he came like a cloud, either in the spring of 1891 or on the Fourth of July. His command was exact and exacting: Do no harm to anyone, Do right always.[10]

Various tribes reacted differently to Wovoka's ghost dance. Some gave up fighting; others retreated to the mountains to await the flood that would wipe out the white men; others believed a four-day sleep would overcome believers and on the fifth day they would awaken to a new world; and still others awaited a hurricane that would kill the whites and return the land to the Indians.

Something like this, in a psychological sense, happens in Logan's work. His quarrels, especially those involving sin, his mother's death, and his search for his father's forgiveness, lead to stress, and as the poem is capable of creating only limited catharsis in the act of its creation, Logan forms a sacred community of brothers bonded together in a love of mankind that is capable of breaking down barriers separating "a man from a / man, and the husbands from their wives . . ." (ST, 11). Although Logan's solution to the tug-and-pull of polar influences within himself is certainly not fantasied in the way Wovoka's solution is, it is, nevertheless, a fantasied solution which, like other solutions that attempt to link religion and the pleasure principle in some kind of love of mankind, runs the risk of ritualizing an indiscriminate or "unreal" response to human relationships in the process of alleviating stress and anxiety.

"Lines on His Birthday," for example, dramatizes Logan's feelings that his father's death might make his remorse greater rather than less, and the tone of the poem seems tense and abrupt, and even Logan's powerful lyricism has been cut to the bone. In response to these kinds of tensions, these quarrels, he recreates, as he says, "in his work the body of his mother . . . [and] he wishes to give birth to her as she has done for him" (V, 19), and he transforms the anxiety associated with his mother's death into a ritual of forgiveness

> . . . that charms the exile
> of listeners into a bond of brothers, breaking
> down the lines of lead that separate a man from a
> man, and the husbands from their wives, in these old, burned
>   glass
> panels of our lives.   (ST, 11)

The transformation of the guilt from his mother's death (including his ambivalent feelings about his father from whom he has to seek forgiveness) into a healing and transcendent love is one of Logan's recurring themes. The ghost dance, the ritual, the almost magical solution, changes the exiled listeners, including himself, from lonely and anonymous people into a bond of brothers which offers love and hope rather than the despair of guilt and shame. By creating this body, this community of brothers, Logan is able to refashion his environment. He transforms guilt and remorse into a brotherly love that is, at its best, healing and communal, and, at its worst, self-serving and cruel.

Logan's inheritance has complicated ramifications. What interests me most, though, are the transformations, the rituals that give birth to a kind of ghost dance, a kind of vision which changes tense, ambivalent situations into brotherhoods. These transformation rituals share characteristics with genuine ghost dances where shamans change anxiety-causing situations (i.e., reality or its interpretation) into something more acceptable by magical or fantastical visions. In both *The Zigzag Walk* and *The Anonymous Lover*, Logan creates these magical, healing environments of brotherly love. The former book is peopled with father figures, sons, and brothers; and in the latter, he widens the breadth of his environment to embrace sisters, daughters, and female lovers. In the "Poem: Tears, Spray, and Steam" that concludes *The Anonymous Lover*, Logan describes his and his companions' return to the sulfur baths where

> from our dance along the open shore
> we find the Esalen
>   teacher there again,
> and the watchman,
> each with a woman.
> They wait
>   in that gentle, lunatic light for us.
> They smile as they undress.
> Eric Barker takes a leak,
> begins reciting Keats,
> and we all bathe and sing together
> in the new waters of brother, sister.   (AL, 84)

These soothing "new waters" are the kinds of places that Logan creates in his search for forgiveness, love, and solace. His "use" of poetry as a ghost dance ritual brings people together, but it also has the opposite power, the power of cruelty and aggression to transform reality into a self-serving environment disguised under the cloak of love and communion. As he writes in "Letter To A Young Father in Exile":

> And finally this, my own thoughtless role:
> you write me a note
>   about your first son,
> a bastard like the rare and brilliant one
> of St. Augustine,
> and in my brief reply I do not even
> mention
>   him. Well, I see (sadly) I am cruel.
> And I too know how to kill!
> For when I last wrote
> and said I wanted to forget
>   (abort
> your image out of my mind)
> simply because you are not around
> for my solace and my life, now
> I see raised what came
>   into my hand
> against you. Thus

I am loving and as treacherous
as parent or as child—in the black
ancient figure you and he may fight to break.
Oh my lost, abandoned brother,
you know you had a father.   (ZW, 116)

Brotherly love transforms, it creates solace, and it can suffocate. In his search for solace and forgiveness, Logan takes the posture of a charismatic wanderer who, on one hand, is concerned mostly with himself— for brotherly love is, at one extreme, a self-serving ritual which highlights one aspect of reality (e.g., personal solace) over others (e.g., communal work ethics)—, and who, on the other hand, is a part of the loving, healing community he has created. The poet thus becomes a father who fashions an environment from his unconscious mind. The environment is made not only from love but also from instinctual aggression— the same aggression that gives rise to the conflicts of parents, families, and cultures where fathers, the "maleness" of our selves, "breed stern standards and the necessity for actively earning approval."[11]   These standards and the search for approval (or forgiveness?) usually lead to confrontations and conflict. The conflicts (between fathers and sons, mothers and fathers, etc.) can be resolved through love and patience, as Logan's often are, but are, often enough, resolved through aggressive or cruel acts. Although we may be shameful of these cruelties (as Logan is with his response to the young father in exile), they have to be dealt with openly rather than denied or repressed, or else we run the risk of creating a truly fantastical, lopsided reality that presents human relationships as all love and solace (or the opposite). In Logan's case, aggression, especially when it addresses his relationships with his father, gets absorbed into sex and love, as it does here in this first section of his ambitious and compelling "Poem in Progress," which is one of the few instances where he allows himself to express his violent feelings. Here is the section of this poem where his aggressions come through in an image of reckless driving.

I think of that possible slip
out of the ship's fastenings
into the long sleep of the wake.
But I wave though. I try to greet,
as the boat moves on quietly through the avenues,
some aging men on corners in this alien place.
But they only talk among themselves. How can they miss
this ship in the streets, these old men—
miss *me* trying to salute them? Father, I suppose
it's you again. Why did you stop
hunting for the vivid pheasants in the fields
or having a beer with your friends

in the old Westerlund Cafe
when I was young in Red Oak, Iowa? Oh, I once
thought we might have talked, might try to have something to say.
Instead I ran my buddy's car ninety miles an hour
down Highway 48 outside of town and jacked off
when I got home. Father, I love you still—
still yearn for your advice. Shall I turn back toward the tip
of the ship? There are people alive close by upstairs
in this many-tiered boat. I can hear them as the ageless, orange
                                                    moon ri-
ses over the small hill or houses. Well, I will go
up there to the sailors perhaps
or the families or the whores—
whoever *lives* on this ghosted ship that floats through the streets
where absolutely anything goes, and there *are* no shores.
                                                    (BC, 31-2)

Later in the same long poem, in section VI titled "Union: Father,
Son, Friend, Archetype," Logan identifies the ties of his brotherhood
as "that generative giving" between "Friends, / father and son, bro-
thers" who balance their burdens and gifts to create the kind of envir-
onment that offers pleasure and solace in place of violence and despair.

The waves rushed in again—still. You'd made love with your girl,
you said, here, this very place, in the warmer New Year.
One of the deeper bright planes of the waves was that one—
that generative giving. Friends,
father and son, brothers, we clung
together, digging our feet deep into the black soil
of the sea's hill, burrowing back
in the cave of our bodies molded
as if to feel in touch with the earth that binds us all
together and keeps us from blowing away in those
powerful winds that will fill and shake at us always,
at the old man hill with its veins of time like frozen
waves upon waves. It was as if we were his own poised
burden and gift, the young man born out of the older
or the old from the young, the two of us planted there
together beside the loud sea . . .   (BC, 40)

In the earlier fifth section of "Poem in Progress" Logan describes a
Colombian Statue as an archetype for the kind of balancing and bridg-
ing of opposites he finds so necessary and compelling:

The Colombian fellow is bearded, benevolent, hatted, a sack—
like some kind of load—at his back, and the jutting folds

of his cloak like two, low wings. He carries a big bag
of gold or of fish in his, say, fifty-year-old hands
(or he's pregnant with it, with the gift which balances
perfectly the weight on his back).
This bag's tied up in some cloth that looks knotted in front.
His beard parts above the pursed mouth of the sack: the breath
he has breathed into it—or it has blown inside him—
is given back again. In him, old Colombian,
the love of fulfillment he offers us matches ex-
actly at his back the love of lack.　　　　　　　　　(BC, 38)

This, "say, fifty-year-old" Colombian strikes me as a characteristic sym-
bol for Logan's poetry. Like Logan, he offers "the love of fulfillment"
along with "the love of lack." The polar influences are metaphorically
balanced in a primal scene that projects a pregnancy ("or he's pregnant
with it, with the gift which balances") onto the archetype; and from
this pregnant posture, the archetype creates a balance that gives Logan
the occasion for creating a poem. *The Bridge of Change*, Logan's most
recent full-length collection which includes "Poem in Progress," dwells
on the notions of balance and bridge. Like these examples from "Poem
in Progress," the predominate metaphor in this book, the balancing and
bridging of opposites, takes its cue from the epigraph taken from Rilke
for the title poem, "The Bridge of Change"–"The bridge barely curved
that connects / the terrible with the tender" (BC, 49). After describing
some quite incredible historic and present-day Parisian scenes, including
a young fire-eater, Logan concludes "The Bridge of Change" with this
last section.

Who can stand these juxtapositions of person and place and time?
I walk across the Bridge of Change where I have so often watched
by the towers of the Conciergerie. Now, water laves a little higher
up the stair from the River to the Quay, hiding some of the steps
from me. Boats nudge at the edge. I walk along the Boulevard
past the great gold and blue corner clock, the ornate wrought-
iron gate and fence of the Place of Justice, (its name changed
from the time of kings), past the shadow and spire of Sainte Cha-
pelle. I cross the Bridge of Saint Michel into the Latin Quarter.
But I do not look for the Street of the Cat Who Fishes or the
Street of the Harp. I turn right, wandering a bit, and suddenly,
as if by chance, find myself at *this* street, and here I will wait,
for it is our street, *Rue Gît le Coeur: Here Lies the Heart*.
　　　　　　　　　　　　　　　　　　　　　(BC, 53)

After crossing the bridge of change, literally and metaphorically, Logan
wanders, crosses other bridges, and by chance finds himself at Rue Gît
le Coeur. The heart, source of the bond of brothers, *is* Logan's street.

114

As he says here in his essay on poetry and poets, this bond, this charming of exiled listeners in this personal ghost dance has the almost magical power of bridging the gaps between listeners and readers and thus brings them together so they feel "neither alone nor anonymous" even though they may be both.

> Poets say they want everybody to love everybody but they (we) mainly want you the audience to care about us, and so we do what we can to make you feel that we care about you. The poet is an anonymous lover I believe, and his poetry is an anonymous reaching out, which occasionally becomes personal—when there are those present who care to listen. At the personal moment a mysterious thing happens, which reminds us of magic, and hence of the power of Orpheus: the loneliness each of us feels locked inside his own skin, and the anonymous reaching each of us does therefore, becomes a *bond* and hence we are neither alone nor anonymous in the same sense as we were before.
>
> (V, 23)

Finally, it is Logan's ghost dance, his ritualistic, almost magical charming of each of us into a brotherhood where he, the poet, is father, son and brother at once that comforts us, that teaches us how to hold off despair in an impersonal world. Through his balancing and bridging, through his quarrels with himself, and through the gift of his voice, he dramatizes his concerns for others, for personal relationships, for us his readers. To help us with our burdens, he offers the occasions to enter his poems where pain and grief are transformed into pleasure and love. This is his ghost dance. This is his gift.

Notes

[1] Logan cites this phrase in "John Logan on Poets and Poetry Today," *Voyages*, IV, nos. 3-4 (1972), p. 21. I use the following abbreviations in the essay for works by Logan: *Cycle For Mother Cabrini* (New York, 1955), CMC; *Ghosts of the Heart* (Chicago, 1960), GH; *Spring of the Thief* (New York, 1963), ST; *The Zigzag Walk* (New York, 1969), ZW; *The Anonymous Lover* (New York, 1973), AL; *The Bridge of Change* (Brockport, New York, 1981), BC; "John Logan on Poets and Poetry Today," *Voyages*, IV, nos. 3-4 (1972), 17-24, V.

[2] Charles Altieri, "Poetry as Resurrection: John Logan's Structures of Metaphysical Solace," *Modern Poetry Studies*, 3 (1973), 193-224, points to the changes in Logan's poetry over the course of his career up until 1973. Although we approach Logan's poetry from different perspectives, Altieri's fine essay is the source of my thinking about enduring themes in Logan's work, including the thief metaphor.

[3] Sigmund Freud, *The Ego and the Id*, trans. Joan Riviere, rev. by James Strachey (New York, 1960), pp. 18-30.

[4] Weston La Barre, *The Ghost Dance: The Origins of Religion* (New York, 1970), p. 15.

[5] Sigmund Freud, *Civilization and Its Discontents*, trans. James Strachey (New York, 1961), p. 49.

[6] *Civilization and Its Discontents*, p. 49.

[7] *The Ghost Dance*, p. 46.

[8] *The Ghost Dance*, p. 15.

[9] *The Ghost Dance*, p. 48.

[10] *The Ghost Dance*, pp. 229-30.

[11] *The Ghost Dance*, p. 104.

© 1984 Mary Randlett

John Logan inside poet Robert Sund's little red house on Ravenna
Avenue N.E., Seattle, April 14, 1966.

A Communication Among the Faithful

TAMA BALDWIN

John Logan has written several poems in praise of other writers—
Rilke, Joyce, Thomas, Yeats, Cummings. It becomes clear that these
"homages" are not simply gestures of reverence; these poems also trace
their way through the sensibilities of earlier writers. Logan is creating
his own tradition, and it is built on writers who share with him a passion
for the primacy of language. It is the *presentation* of the shades and
textures of individual experience, rather than *re-presentation*, that is
their artistic concern. They know well that the rhythm, sound, and
resonance of the word must be yoked to the context in a way that will
startle the reader into recognition.

An illumination of this language-life connection can be found in
Logan's relationship with the work of the French playwright-novelist
Jean Giraudoux. In an interview with Dan Murray (1968), Logan men-

tions his appreciation of Giraudoux's anti-naturalist work. He is especially attracted to the dramatist's artistic philosophy; both men emphasize the transforming power of language. Giraudoux and his ally, director Louis Jouvet, defied naturalist dramatists by declaring language the most important element of drama. Giraudoux believed that with words he could form a bond with the audience that was both intimate and anonymous—much like the relationship between priest and parishoner. "Theater," writes Giraudoux, "is like a Catholic mass of the language."[1] And a belief in the necessity of a verbal communion is at the core of Logan's poetics. Robert Cohen helpfully paraphrases Giraudoux and Jouvet's desire for this secular marriage: "Jouvet writes of the theater as a *fidèle entretien*, implying a communication among the faithful. It is a 'passionate contract, a communion, a joint participation, a reciprocal interpenetration.' "[2] Their drama, Cohen continues, "is a lay religion in which the metaphysical struggles of human life could be played out in theatrical ceremony."[3]

The histories that members of the audience bring to the playhouse are prodded by the music of the language as well as by the struggles the words depict. The drama is successful when a moment of recognition occurs; when the pulse begins to accelerate and the skin starts to tingle, the observer becomes witness—to something within himself; a physiologic knowing deeper and more certain than an intellectual apprehension occurs. Logan has expressed many times his belief that poetry can provide this relationship, a union he describes as "anonymous loving."

For Logan, all settings contain potential material for a poem: the mass, the corner bar, a party, the beach, a museum. Often, in fact, the most unlikely places and situations provide him with the occasion for poetry. This receptivity is reflected not only in his selection of images but also in his use of language. Frequently, he uses the most ordinary words and, with his lyrical gift, brings them into the sphere of music. In "Homage to Rainer Maria Rilke," Logan concurs with Rilke that all words possess the potential to become the transfiguring element in poetry:

> I love the poor, weak words
> which starve in daily use—
> the ordinary ones.
> With the brush of my breath
> I color them. They brighten then
> and grow almost gay.
> They have never known
> melody before who trem-
> bling step into my song.

Profane as well as commonplace words help build a Logan poem. The lyricism of the close of "Three Moves" partially reflects a self-conscious irony, but it is also peculiar and touching.

Oh these ducks are all right.
They will survive.
But I am sorry I do not often see them climb.
Poor sons-a-bitching ducks.
You're all fucked up.
What do you do that for?
Why don't you hover near the sun anymore?
Afraid you'll melt?
These foolish ducks lack a sense of guilt,
and so all their multi-thousand-mile range
is too short for the hope of change.

Logan's use of the 'ordinary' words, as well as the profane and the cliché, does not make his verse simply prosaic, though it is easy to mistake the casualness such language can evoke as just that. But he has applied the poet's gift of finding sound and stress relationships within the line and between the lines to alter simultaneously the language and the experience. When he is successful, as in "Three Moves," an effective tension surfaces which modulates these 'ordinary' words into a resonance of sound and meaning they wouldn't have in an everyday context.

Logan's selected poems offer all kinds of wealth, and one of the most provocative examples of the richness is in his use of language. *Only The Dreamer Can Change The Dream* offers a compendium of ways to find musical relationships in the line. In particular, Logan's use of the hyphenated line break is a revealing part of his poetics. Ever since his first book he has broken lines in the middle of words. Frequently, the hyphenated line breaks demonstrate Logan's attempt to exploit subtleties of meaning. Logan often explores the function of a word's etymology. The etymologies of "amplify," "musical," and "confuse," for example, refer specifically to the perception and enrich meaning.

I mean the gift of the structure of a poet's jaw,
which makes the mask that's cut out of the flesh of his face
a megaphone—as with the goat clad Greeks—to ampli-
fy the light gestures of his soul toward the high stone seats.

("To A Young Poet Who Fled")

I looked deep into a pool
of blue water—we had no mirror—and I was so
amazed I looked over my shoulder, for I did not
imagine it was me, caught
in that cerulean sky.

John Logan at Daniela Gioseffi's house, Brooklyn, Heights, New York, February 27, 1974.

> Thinking it was someone other, I tell you I con-
> fused myself with my brother!
>
> ("Poem For My Brother")

> This artist's sculptured, open box of mahogany
> (ivory white inside) is strung
> with vertical and horizontal layers of mus-
> ical wires that sing when struck, and bits of bright garnet
> rock tremble where they intersect.
> These gems flash in the candle light,
> and before me all my beloved childhood looms up
> in the humming levels, each one deeper than the other.
>
> ("Grace")

These line breaks also create an unexpected sort of onomatopoeia. Often, the forced duration of particular sounds enables the word to more closely resemble its meaning. The sense-extension of these words under the stress of their position is evoked: "breath- / less," "sun- / ken," "scat- / tering," "o- / ver," and "trem- / ble."

Logan's agile use of the hyphenated line break is only a part of his search for an authentic style. He often uses the end of a line to find "new musical relationships." The end rhymes he uses sometimes startle when he hyphenates a word to find in it a thyme that is semantically important.

> We all live
> > on islands.
> And you and I've
> > wand-
> ered far this day
> on one . . . .
>
> ("Poem for My Friend Peter at Pihana")

Here he sets up an effective spatial relationship between "island" and "wand- / ered," but he finds as well multiplicity of meaning. The speaker wanders the island: its terrain and its history; and he calls also upon a magic the beauty of the place provides to sustain him as he confronts a crisis within himself; the place possesses power. Logan often uses such unpredictable rhymes that discover the music in usually 'mute' words. He is very aware that "most rhyme in contemporary poetry has so much echo to it of nineteenth-century work or early twentieth-century work that it's very hard to hear the voice of a contemporary poet behind rhymes which, just as rhythms and expressions, can be cliché."[4]

Logan's poems have become more bold in their confrontation of a man's spiritual struggles and this change seems to have occurred along with an increasing experimentation with tradition. He appears to have found that the ten syllable line he uses so naturally in earlier poems like "The Brothers: Two Saltimbanques," "Concert Scene," or "New York Scene: May 1958" is not suited to the more personal lyrics of recent books. After *Ghosts of the Heart* (1960) he never again—with the exception of a few sections of poems—uses decasyllabic verse as a standard. His new line constructions seem to be premised upon a wariness of the cliché, the strong echoes of a tradition that can no longer be of use to him. The spiritual chaos he confronts in his poems possesses an emotional texture that would be distorted by more conventional rhythms. In *The Bridge of Change* there are quite a few 7/13 syllable line combinations, as in these lines from "Poem For My Brother":

> I loved my brother, but never quite knew what to think.
> For example, he would beat
> me up as soon as the folks
> left the house, and I would cry big, loud feminine tears.
> He was good at sports and played football, and so instead
> I was in the marching band.
> My brother stole rubbers from the store and smoked cigars
> and pipes, which made me sick. But

Quietly present here is the ten syllable line. He has fractured the decasyllabic into a 13 syllable line of excess and a 7 syllable line of constraint. When the lines are coupled the equivalent of two ten syllable lines are present and provide an underlying sense of potential order. He never completely departs from the standard; he modifies it for his use. The rhythm created by the over-reaching and short-striding lines produces a number of effects. The sense of labored breathing and a searching rhythm play their part in the context of spiritual struggle that weaves through the poems.

Logan frequently cites Nietzsche's description of a poem: "the vision generated by the dance." And his poems, for all their semantic power, are also sound rituals; he believes the poet can heal with his musing and his music:

> I mean the gift of the structure of a poet's jaw
> which makes the mask that's cut out of the flesh of his face
> a megaphone—as with the goat clad Greeks—to ampli-
> fy the light gestures of his soul toward the high stone seats.
> The magic of the mouth that can melt to tears the rock
> of hearts. I mean the wand of tongues that charms the exile
> of listeners into a bond of brothers, breaking
> down the lines of lead that separate a man from a

man, and the husbands from their wives, in these old, burned glass
panels of our lives.

("To A Young Poet Who Fled")

Logan believes, like Giraudoux, the magic of language soothes as it
evokes, at least briefly, the pain of the birth-imposed alienation that is
part and parcel of individuality.

For Logan, the search through poetry for a "momentary peace"—a
phrase of Dylan Thomas's he cites often—is his means of supplement-
ing, if not replacing, a grace offered by conventional Christian cere-
mony. Logan has connected poetry and piety many times in his essays
and interviews, and a number of Logan's poems present the voice of a
man discontent with the church. In "Spring of the Thief," the speaker
of the poem has grown melancholy at the Mass's "ancient story / of
the unclean ghost / a man thought he'd lost." He arrives at a church in
a time of need but finds it locked. He troubles over the fact that "The
name of God is changing in our time. / What is his winter name?" The
conventional emphasis upon the sin and shame within can no longer
provide him with that necessary grace: *Blessed be sin if it teaches men
shame.* / Yet because of it we cannot talk / and I am separated from
myself." By the poem's close he has found a new, liberating name for
God:

> Ekelöf said there is a freshness
> nothing can destroy in us—
> not even we ourselves.
> Perhaps that
> *Freshness* is the changed name of God.

He chooses to place emphasis upon beauty that exists concordant with
ugliness:

> Where all the monsters also hide
> I bear him in the ocean of my blood
> and in the pulp of my enormous head.
> He lives beneath the unkempt potter's grass
> of my belly and chest.
> I feel his terrible, aged heart
> moving under mine . . . can see the shadows
> of the gorgeous light
> that plays at the edges of his giant eye . . .
> or tell the faint press and hum
> of his eternal pool of sperm.

Many of Logan's poems attempt this kind of affirmation; the lushness
of the verse carries his belief in some sort of over-ruling goodness or
potential. And his renovation of a traditional poetics is intimately

related to his search for grace in the nontraditional, secular ceremony of his poetry.

For Logan, experience and memory are no longer a part of life he must dispense with through confession. Rather, they become the source of poetry. He achieves grace through imagination and with the music of his language. The apparently autobiographical tone and imagery of his poetry can be misleading; the voice that wishes to touch the reader is, finally, that of a transformed man—anonymous in that he possesses no exact history but exists only in the present of the poem. All that Logan may be is brought to the moment of writing, but in the poems he finds a kind of lyrical objectivity about his condition. The reaching beyond the particular self, beyond blindingly distinct human ties, is precipitated by a common yearning, an anxiety he chooses to inhabit in order to know more.

"Poem: Tears, Spray, and Steam" makes explicit Logan's belief in the lay religion of poetry. Bathing naked in the hot springs, the speaker, friends, and strangers begin a Dionysian ritual under the moon. The setting—the springs, with their rich history—serves as a potent metaphor. According to legend, the mountain is the transformed body of a grief-stricken Indian prince who died because he feared his rituals could not heal his ailing sister:

> But in that warm spring
> water which we briefly left, everything
>
> > eventually heals:
>
> . . . .
> . . . And everybody here who comes together
>
> > in belief
> is somehow bound, bathed,
>
> > and made
> whole, e-
> > ven as was she
> by this gradual, glinting water,
> the prince's continual tears for his sister.

Reading Keats, they all "bathe and sing together / in the new waters of brother, sister." The prince's mortal grief becomes a restorative bath—first for his sister and then for the bathers. And Keats's poems—born out of pain like the water—wash and unite them as well. They become lovers in their spiritual union when they enter the *new* primordial waters. These faithful celebrants find in their moment of communion a sweet, temporary peace.

A number of Logan's more recent poems incorporate the poetic process into the narrative. Often, the reader is invoked as an integral part of the narrator's search:

124

And I must not be alone
no matter what needs be done,
for then my search is ended.
So now the panicked thumbs of my poem pick
through the grill. They poke
the lock
and put out a hand and then an arm.
The limbs of my poems
come within your reach.
Perhaps it is you whom I seek.

("The Search")

In "Assateague" the poet-narrator "explains" the context of the poem;
in an introductory stanza he anticipates the search for communion that
occurs in the body of the poem:

Tamar and Royce are in love.
They run up the beach and give
each other a hand. I walk
behind and brood. I'll try my luck:

The island, initially a desolate setting, "Grey the sky and grey the sea,"
is finally transformed by the poet into an element of unification, like
the springs at Big Sur in "Poem: Tears, Spray, and Steam." The indige-
nous, wild ponies provide an exact metaphor for our own birth-imposed
isolation:

. . . The round-up is harsh
yearly, decimates the herds
driven before the waves and winds:

They swim across the channel
goaded by the boys and men
and up the beach into pens
pattering up over moist sands

and dashing the placid salt
pools into myriad drops.
Roped and with spirits broken,
the ponies are driven inland

and for the rest of their bound
lives they yearn for salt and sedge
they fed on under the ridge
of snow along the island edge

125

as we yearn for our childhood
or the love we never had
or else had but could not keep
until we came to Assateague.

On the island, yearning is eased. The lovers join hands, and their union brings them peace, even though they have no knowledge of the poet's imaginative act. Like the lovers in Dylan Thomas's "In My Craft or Sullen Art," they have no need of the poet's art. Still the poet satisfies himself by singing of their love:

Not for the proud man apart
From the raging moon I write
On these spindrift pages
Nor for the towering dead
With their nightingales and psalms
But for the lovers, their arms
Round the griefs of the ages,
Who pay no praise or wages
Nor heed my craft or art.

The lovers possess, as Logan discovers in his "Elegy for Dylan Thomas," "the solace of the living": touch. Peace for them is articulated through the flesh. The poet finds "the solaces of art": image and sound. The first stanza of "Assateague," which at first seems out of sync with the narrative flow, finally provides the poem with a complexity that enables it to become far more than a sentimental anecdote. For Logan, peace is articulated through imagistic complexity and sound; the poem becomes communion.

Notes

[1] Jean Giraudoux, *Littérature*, trans. Robert Cohen, in his critical study *Giraudoux: Three Faces of Destiny* (Chicago and London: University of Chicago Press, 1968), p. 137.

[2] Cohen, p. 134.

[3] Cohen, p. 140.

[4] John Logan, *A Ballet for the Ear*, ed. A. Poulin, Jr. (Ann Arbor: The University of Michigan Press, 1983), p. 17.

Bibliography

Cohen, Robert. *Giraudoux: Three Faces of Destiny*. Chicago and London: The University of Chicago Press, 1968.
Giraudoux, Jean. *Littérature*. Paris: Éditions Bernard Grasset, 1941.

Logan, John. *A Ballet for the Ear*. Ann Arbor: The University of Michigan Press, 1983.

_____. *The Bridge of Change*. Brockport: BOA Editions, 1981.

_____. *Only The Dreamer Can Change The Dream*. New York: The Ecco Press, 1981.

Thomas, Dylan. *Collected Poems*. New York: New Directions, 1957.

The Resurrecting Act: John Logan's Poems on Literary Figures

DAVID WOJAHN

In the opening section of the title poem of John Logan's first volume, *Cycle for Mother Cabrini*, the poet pays homage to his subject by visiting her resting place, and is thus given the opportunity to both enumerate the saint's accomplishments and compare his own imperfect and sinful existence to her life of piety. As in so many of Logan's later poems, this meditation is accompanied less by agonized self-questioning than by an almost childlike sense of awe and wonder. The most memorable devotional literature, Logan seems to be telling us, strives for an innocent personal receptivity. While the concerns of Logan's early religious poetry were abandoned after his break with Catholicism in the 1960s, Logan's attitude toward the devotional experience has remained unchanged, and it has been a guiding principle in nearly all of his poems. James Dickey, in a 1962 review of Logan's second volume, *Ghosts of the Heart*, characterized him as a poet of "sacramental relationships" and this label continues to be an accurate one. Logan's best mature poems record the events and experiences which he has now come to regard as sacramental: intimacy between lovers, moments of communion during friendship, and encounters with art and literature. Logan seeks to elevate such experience to the level of the devotional and sacramental through honest personal disclosure and a keen sense of narrative and dramatic values. While Logan's attempts to achieve this goal in his most forthrightly intimate poems on love and friendship are sometimes marred by sentimentality, his poems on literary figures—though often incorporating autobiographical material—rarely suffer from this shortcoming. Through homage, elegy, and the devotional act of pilgrimage, Logan seeks to "canonize" those writers whose work has been important to him. Read chronologically, Logan's poems on other writers reflect the development of his work from poetry of strained and sometimes excessively literary religiosity to the more straightforwardly autobiographical efforts of his mature phase. In many ways, Logan's poems on literary figures are among the most "personal" he has written.

The problem of finding the right means to incorporate autobiography into their work has been a major concern for the poets of Logan's generation, most of whom began to publish in the 1950s. While some of Logan's contemporaries, following the lead of Lowell, Sexton, and the other Confessional poets, used the most intimate and harrowing personal revelations to achieve a tentative catharsis, others, most notably Wright and Simpson in the early '60s, sought to combine purely autobiographical writing with the irrational and highly subjective imagery of surrealism, seeking a sort of shadowy self-transcendence. Logan's poems, while growing increasingly concerned with personal subject matter throughout the '60s, seem little influenced by either of these approaches. His poems never seek self-confrontation for its own sake in the lurid manner in which the later poems of Sexton do; Logan's self-examinations usually occur before and during the sacramental moments of experiencing love, friendship, or art and literature, and we therefore see in them little of the alienation so predominant in confessional verse. In even his most introspective efforts—such as the well-known "Three Moves," from *The Zigzag Walk*— Logan is *never* alone. He invariably addresses an audience of intimates which the Confessional poets in their most extreme efforts deny exists. (*Who* is Lowell speaking to in "Skunk Hour," or Berryman in Dream Song #384? Both poems achieve their effect in part because the writers presuppose that the intended audience may not be able to listen.) In a gesture typical of Logan's poetry, "Three Moves" contains an aside addressed directly to the reader ("Who / will forgive me then? Will you?") and concludes with a whimsical, but also self-mocking harangue addressed to the ducks who swim beyond the poet's houseboat. Logan's response to a lack of audience, in this case, is simply to *invent* one. Just as the stance of alienation essential to Confessional verse is antithetical to Logan's temperament, Surrealism is equally out of place in his approach, for Surrealism's emphasis is on subjective disclosure rather than intimate disclosure. The nuances of the poet's dialogue between his conscious and unconscious is generally more important to him than his engagement with the exterior world. Logan's goal of intimacy cannot ascribe to Surrealism's solipsism and ambiguity. More open-hearted than perhaps any of the poets of his generation, Logan has nothing to hide, and therefore nothing to confess, and nothing that he experiences prompts him to turn inward. His is a poetry of intimacy because he has from the very beginning of his career made a pact with his reader that causes the poems to be both sweetly tender and exasperating: Logan idealizes his reader, trusts him completely. Though we sometimes grow uncomfortable in our role as confidants, feeling that perhaps we have been told more about Logan than we would prefer to know, we nonetheless feel special, each of us chosen for an almost sacred role.

Perhaps because Logan so adamantly refuses to posture before his audience, to wear any sort of mask, his poems on literary figures have increasingly sought to eschew mannerisms, and to avoid the "literary" as much as possible. In his Keats elegy, or in his recent elegy for Dylan Thomas, he speaks to the poets in the same way he speaks to us—informally, revealingly, and yet with great intensity. The language of these poems is conversational in part because Logan rejects the elevated diction of mourning and mere homage. He addresses his literary figures from a stance of gratitude and thanksgiving. This does not mean, however, that he refuses to judge his poets' lives and work—his poems on Hart Crane and Rimbaud, for example, are markedly ambivalent in their attitudes towards these figures and their writing. But, curiously, the poems of Logan which are most critical of their literary subjects are often the least successful. When Logan approaches his subjects in unquestioning wonder, as he approached the bones of Mother Cabrini in his first collection, then we see Logan's best work, for he insists on portraying his writers in the same unaffected way in which he portrays himself. The more his literary portraiture is accompanied by self-portraiture, the more satisfying it becomes. Logan himself understood this early in his career, as evidenced by the following comments made during a 1961 interview with Marvin Bell:

> The turning point came when, after writing about Heine and Rimbaud (I wrote about Byron, Shelley, James Joyce, and Hart Crane later), I became faced concretely with the problem of dealing with a live artist—myself.

Logan's poems on literary figures fall into three general periods: the early monologues and dramatic poems which appear in *Cycle for Mother Cabrini* and *Ghosts of the Heart*, the discursive biographical poems which also appear in *Ghosts of the Heart*, and finally the most mature of Logan's poems from literary sources, the autobiographical poems of pilgrimage from *The Zigzag Walk* and Logan's most recent collection, *The Bridge of Change*. These categories do not include Logan's poems from literary *sources*, such as "Monologues of the Son of Saul" in *Spring of the Thief*, his verse retelling of Melville's *Pierre* in *The Zigzag Walk*, nor his idiosyncratic adaptations of some of Rilke's poems included in the same volume. Neither does this grouping include the many meditations on works of art which Logan has published over the years—his numerous poems on photographs by Aaron Siskind, for example. But the poems I wish to discuss, "The Death of Southwell" from *Cycle*, "The Lives of the Poet," Logan's study of Rimbaud, from *Ghosts*, "On the Death of Keats," from *Zigzag*, and "Elegy for Dylan Thomas," from *The Bridge of Change*, clearly chart the process of Logan's development.

Robert Southwell, minor Elizabethan poet and Catholic priest and martyr, is a fitting subject for the earliest of Logan's poems on literary figures. Imprisoned by Anglican authorities in 1592 for surreptitiously administering the sacraments to British Catholics, Southwell was hanged in Tyburn in 1595. Subtitled "A Verse Melodrama with Homilies on Light and Sin," the poem is more distinguished for its promise than for its accomplishment. Its narrative is confused, and its language is often stilted. At times Logan seems to be imitating the clotted syntax of the early Robert Lowell, who Logan has spoken of as an important early influence. At other times, Logan rather unconvincingly attempts to duplicate Elizabethan diction, as in Southwell's long speech near the end of the poem. Combining narrative, discursive, and dramatic elements, without maintaining the consistent point of view found in Logan's later poems, "The Death of Southwell" is largely an academic exercise, despite—and perhaps because of—its ambitions. Jarrell's reservation about some of the writing in Lowell's *The Mills of the Kavanaughs* might also apply to the Southwell poem. We see Logan "having to try much too hard, so that one does not feel very often . . . the spontaneity, the live half-accidental, half-providential rightness, that some of the best poetry has or seems to have." "The Death of Southwell" is a poem made up mostly of *effects*, yet these effects are interesting and varied, and in some cases predict what is to follow in Logan's later poetry.

While the poem's initial stanza, which sets the scene for Southwell's arrest by Topcliffe, contains some awkward moments (". . . the candles/ Too drawn, their flames rest-/ Less ruddying the cup"), stanza two has some of the cinematic precision of descriptive passages in Logan's more recent work:

> Topcliffe's horses shake
> The steam of gray morning; men
> Grow sad with cold.
> The house is sketched well-marked
> Where Mass is said. What argument?
> The traitor's vested. Take him.
> Cloak his colors! These horses
> Scream. Now load his books,
> His papist images; and this
> Damned altar furniture
> That burnishes with sun!

But the stanzas that follow, which contain a description of Southwell's imprisonment and torture on the rack and a delirious speech of Southwell's drawn in part from phrases from his poem "The Burning Babe," are plodding and diffuse. While they seem to strive for the same particularity of detail found in stanza two, they have none of the earlier stanza's clarity and immediacy. It is only in stanza eight that the poem recovers its momentum, for suddenly the speaker, without warning, interjects commentary. This technique has not been used in the poem before, and at first seems out of place. Up until this point, Logan has sought to glorify Southwell, but now he belittles his subject's poetic achievement. The frankness of the speaker's appraisal causes us to sympathize with Southwell in a manner that has not occurred before:

> He knew he'd hang, and the rest.
> He was always very white of face.

What falconry he had he
Put in poems. Uneasy in disguise.
No champion. In fact quite
Unfavorably compares to Campion.
A slight man, a poet pulled
Into the common prose of crowds . . .

Unfortunately, what soon follows are Southwell's final words, the homily on light and sin promised in the poem's subtitle. Because of its mock-Shakespearian tone, it contains perhaps too much poetry to be convincing as poetry, and is imbued with a complex liturgical symbolism. The speech goes on for three stanzas, until we come close to wishing that the hangman would perform his duty with more dispatch. Yet the poem's final stanza is both masterful and surprising. Except for its final line, it is written in unpunctuated capitals, and its couplets are far more convincingly Elizabethan than is Southwell's speech. The passage unfolds with a strident music:

HANGMAN SITS IN TYBURN TREE
PREACHER SAYS HIS HOMILY
NOW HIS CART IS PULLED EMPTY
HANGMAN HANGED HIM AWKWARDLY
LOOK THE PREACHER'S HAND IS FREE
BLESSES HANGMAN BLESSES ME
HERE'S A FRIEND TO PULL THE KNEE
GHOST NOW LEAVES HIS YOUNG BODY
THIS POET SAINT WAS THIRTY-THREE
THE HANGMAN MOANS IN TYBURN TREE
NOW UNBLESS HANGMAN, UNBLESS ME.

It is not simply the boldness of the accentuals that gives the passage its urgency; it is also the fact that a first-person speaker appears once again in the poem. In taking on the role of spectator in the final stanza, Logan underscores the poem's themes of guilt and redemption, and gives the poem's final passage a greater degree of dramatic immediacy. By shifting the poem's final emphasis away from Southwell and to the speaker and audience who survive him, Logan reiterates the poem's didactic purpose: we are not encountering a mere biographical study, but a story meant to challenge us and give us solace. The poem is not, finally, about Southwell, but about us. Southwell may be the subject of Logan's poem, but we are the subject of Logan's sermon. A skillful sermonizer concludes his argument by exhorting his audience to change its ways, but he must not exhort so shrilly that he alienates his listeners. While Logan's later poems eschew such didacticism for personal disclosure, the "special relationship" which Logan strives to develop between himself and his audience is already present in "The Death of Southwell."

"The Lives of the Poet," Logan's poem about Rimbaud, is the opening poem of *Ghosts of the Heart*, and, in effect, the first of a trilogy that appears at the beginning of the volume. Of the others, "A Century Piece for Poor Heine" duplicates the biographical approach of Logan's Rimbaud poem, while "On the Death of the Poet's Mother Thirty-Three Years Later" is a moving elegy for the mother who died when Logan was one month old. It is through Logan's juxtaposition of his two studies of literary figures with one of his most personal early efforts that the trilogy achieves its resonance, for each of the poems discusses the artist's tragic inability to accomplish the self-transcendence he longs for, and each poem alternately glorifies and denigrates the act of poetic creation. In the poems, redemption is seen not only as the result of religious striving, but also as the overcoming of Freudian determinism: special emphasis is paid to the struggles between Heine and Rimbaud and their hectoring mothers, and "The Death of the Poet's Mother" opens with epigraphs from both St. Augustine and the Freudian A.A. Brill, the latter stating ". . . *poetry too is nothing but an oral outlet.*" In their original order in *Ghosts of the Heart*, the Rimbaud and Heine poems immediately precede "On the Death of the Poet's Mother," but in *Only The Dreamer Can Change The Dream*, Logan's selected poems, "Death" appears between its two companion pieces, as if to further emphasize the poems' interdependence. To discuss "The Lives of the Poet" without also discussing the other poems of the trilogy is to rob the poem of some of its impact.

The basis for the Rimbaud poem is Wallace Fowlie's biography of the poet. More consistent in tone than "On the Death of Southwell" and more discursive in approach, "The Lives of the Poet" is influenced more by the middle period Auden than by the early work of Lowell. Like Auden's homages to Henry James and Freud, the style of the poem is proselike, making use of a loose syllabic line. By dividing the poem into eleven sections, each twelve lines long, Logan can convey a great deal of biographical information without having to use the mannered transitional devices of "The Death of Southwell." This technique also allows Logan to insert his own asides and ruminations. Rather than delivering a sermon, Logan has this time created a lecture with slides, his discourse illustrated by sharply sketched vignettes from Rimbaud's life. The problem with this method is that the poem sometimes grows burdened by its wealth of detail. Many of the sections are static and merely reportorial ("He caught a cold with a circus troupe / In the north. At last he joined the Dutch / And sailed to Java . . ."). A major reason for this shortcoming is that Logan finds it difficult to resolve his ambivalence toward Rimbaud, who rejected religion and propriety for poetry, then poetry for gunrunning. The contradictions of Rimbaud's existence strain the easy pieties with which Logan could approach the character of Southwell. In acknowledging Rimbaud's idiosyncratic genius, Logan discovers that he must also question his own religious and artistic credos. This ambivalence is present even in the poem's opening section, describing Rimbaud's birth and childhood:

> His hour of birth he rolled
> From his pillow to the
> Floor having hoped a somewhat
> Longer trip that day
> Than this brief stay
> From death. Although he fought
> The usual Sunday walk
> To church, Frederick and Arthur
> Hand in hand, Vitalie
> And Isabelle—each with a blue
> Umbrella, Madame at her careful space:
> Christ and thief to life.

When Logan is able to discard both his troubled questionings about Rimbaud's character and the flatness of mere enumeration of the facts of Rimbaud's life, then the poem achieves its best moments, as in this passage describing Rimbaud's return to his mother's house after his abandonment of Verlaine:

> He went home when hurt
> And so his mother won
> In the end. After the Verlaine
> Melodrama he came
> His arm in a sling, and wrote
> *Une Saison en Enfer*
> In the barn (she heard him groan
> And rave like some Saint
> Anthony in his cave) . . . .

Like some of the best of Logan's work, this passage, through the use of fortuitous enjambments and internal and off-rhymes, is technically impressive, yet none of these effects distracts from the descriptive straightforwardness which Logan intends.

Perhaps the most disappointing section of the poem is its final one, which too conveniently shows the speaker resolving his ambivalence toward his subject. While the language of the passage is lyrically impressive, it seems excessively summary and moralizing when compared to the stark immediacy of the conclusion of the Southwell poem. Logan's Catholicism charges in like the cavalry in a B-western:

> He tried in the bird the rule
> Of the snow, the peculiar luck
> Of flutes: so much the worse
> For the boy who flies his home

And god and verse . . .
. . . .
                    And the verse will clutch
And cast. And the apter alchemies
Of God make one change last.

Yet the Rimbaud poem, especially when read with the poems for Heine
and Logan's mother, shows that Logan's purpose in the opening of
Ghosts of the Heart is more than *merely* a literary one. The poem may
not be personal in tone, but we understand that the questions it raises
about art and faith spring from personal necessity.

It seems to me that Logan's most impressive individual collection is
his fourth, *The Zigzag Walk,* published in 1969. The tone of intimacy
that we associate with Logan's best poems is everywhere present. The
writing is fluid and accomplished, and, because of Logan's gradual dis-
illusionment with Catholicism in the 1960s, the issue of faith is dealt
with in a less doctrinaire fashion than before. "On the Death of Keats,"
subtitled "Lines for Those Who Drown Twice," reflects Logan's new-
found temperament and poetic confidence. It is, like the poem on
Cummings which also appears in the volume, one of his most notable
efforts. "On the Death of Keats" also establishes a structural method
which Logan will follow in many of his subsequent poems on literary
figures.

Poems on the dying days of Keats have become something of a cot-
tage industry among contemporary poets. Jorie Graham and Stanley
Plumly have made recent entries into the field, and Amy Clampitt has
composed a lengthy series of Keats elegies. The reasons for this fasci-
nation are understandable, not only because of the renewed interest in
Keats' work among critics, but also because of the poignant story of
Keats' lingering death. The hundred-page deathbed scene in the Bate
biography of Keats brings many readers to tears, and one of the great-
est difficulties a writer faces in elegizing Keats lies in finding the means
to avoid bathos.

But Logan ably avoids the bathetic in "On the Death of Keats." In
part one of the poem, as with the Rimbaud poem, Logan's main goal is
simply to adhere to the facts:

    The doctor made you swallow cupfuls of your blood
    when it came up
    out of your rotten lungs again.
    Your study of medicine
    made you suffer more the movements
    of your death. One tiny fish
    and a piece of black bread
    to control the blood . . .

But unlike "Lives of the Poet," here the factual description never grows

135

superfluous. Logan names the books on Keats' bedside (*Don Juan*, Plato, Jeremy Taylor), and repeats the poet's famous words to his doctor, "How long is this posthumous life of mine to last?" At times the writing grows a bit effusive— "You starved for food / and air. For poetry. For love." "Your eyes grew huge and bright as those / a gentle animal opens to the night"—but such descriptions are always followed by more objective reporting. What makes part one dramatically effective, in fact, is the speaker's inability to maintain the dispassionate tone he strives for. Fueled by this tension, the last lines of the section are among Logan's most haunting:

> All month you heard the sound of water
> weeping in the Bernini fount.
> You asked your friend to lift you up,
> and died so quietly he thought you slept.
> They buried you with Shelley
> at a cold February dawning
> beside his drowned heart
> which had survived a life
> and death of burning.

What follows in part two is even more impressive. Just as Logan pays homage to Mother Cabrini in his earlier poem by visiting her shrine, Logan here seeks out the graves of Keats and Shelley in the Protestant Cemetery in Rome. This pilgrimage is not the blissful and reverent one we might expect, however. Logan and his wife Ruth make their way through the cemetery on a rainy August afternoon, and the poem becomes as much an uneasy meditation on death as it does a homage to Keats. In fact, in order to visit Keats' remains, Logan must first undertake a journey to the underworld, guided by the eerie figure of a gravekeeper in a black rain slicker:

> Since my birth
> I've waited for the terror of this place.
> The gravekeeper in his hooded black
> rubber cloak
> wades ahead of us toward your tomb.
> The streams that shape and change
> along the tender's rubber back
> light in the thunder flash
> into grotesque slits of eyes.
> They see my fright. Ruth's hand
> is cold in my cold hand.

In the concluding passage, Logan does more than simply give his poem greater authority by introducing biographical information. The poem's real power comes from Logan's willingness to identify himself with

Keats. Such a gesture is not the act of hubris we might think it to be, for what Logan seeks to do is confront his own mortality through empathy with Keats' suffering:

> You, Keats, and Shelley and Ruth
> and I all drown again
> away from home
> in this absurd rain of Rome,
> as you once drowned in your own phlegm,
> and I in my poem. I am afraid.
> The gravekeeper waits.
> He raises his black arm.
> He gestures in the black rain. The sky
> moans long.
> His hooded eyes fire again!
> Suddenly I can read the stone
> which publishes your final line:
> Its date is the birthday of my brother!
> "Here lies one whose name was writ on water."
> Oh Keats, the violet. The violet. The violet
> was your favorite flower.

If the aim of autobiographical writing is to enlarge individual experience in such a way that it speaks for the experience of all of us, then I know of no passage in recent American poetry which accomplishes this goal more successfully. It is not only a moving homage to Keats, but a genuinely empathic one. Despite the appropriately funereal pacing of the passage, its display of poetic effects is dizzying: the strange and wonderful gesture of communion with which it begins, the self-deprecating humor, the casual but masterful use of rhyme, iambics and accentuals, the almost visionary description of the gravekeeper, and the risky but absolutely *brilliant* repetition of "the violet." With this poem Logan has left once and for all the realm of bookish literary homages. While no less literary than its predecessors, the poem shows us all that is vital in John Logan's writing.

Similar descriptions of literary pilgrimages appear in Logan's most recent collection, *The Bridge of Change* (1981). In the collection's third and final section, "Traveling," three poems on literary figures appear, and in each we see Logan on pilgrimage to the graves or environs of his masters. "Dublin Suite: Homage to James Joyce" is the longest and most ambitious of the group, but the poem is uneven, alternating between graceful lyric passages and the fussy prose one might find in a Michelin guidebook. The poem's most successful section is its second, "The Library," describing an exhibit of the ancient Book of Kells. Like *Ulysses*, the book creates a universe in microcosm:

> . . . primitive Celtic gods still cast
> up out of their hermetic interior lives strange figures
> which we can all recognize as
> fragments of our inhuman dreams:
> all this is emblazoned here in the unimagined
> and musical colors of a medieval church.
> Ah, friend, look how this Book of Kells
> pictures all our heavens, all our hells.

"At Drumcliffe Churchyard, County Sligo," Logan's description of his visit to Yeats' grave, seems written more from duty than from need, and the poem is slight when compared to other efforts in the section. "Elegy for Dylan Thomas," however, is one of Logan's most successful recent poems, and deserves to be spoken of in some detail.

Less dramatically intense than "On the Death of Keats," more leisurely in its unfolding, the poem refrains from martyrizing Thomas. Like "Lives of the Poet," "Elegy for Dylan Thomas" treats its subject with ambivalence. In one of the essays collected in his *A Ballet for the Ear*, "Dylan Thomas and the Ark of Art," Logan identifies the conflict between life-force and death-instinct that seems to him the abiding issue in Thomas' life and work, and which culminated in the poet's abandonment of writing and his self-destruction. "For Thomas," Logan writes, "the force of destruction is indissolubly bound with that of construction." In light of this observation, it is understandable that Logan has chosen to make "Elegy for Dylan Thomas" not, as in the Keats elegy, a meditation on death, but instead a meditation on the death-wish. During the course of Logan's pilgrimage with a friend to Thomas' graveside, the forces of self-destruction are repeatedly in conflict with the redemptive powers of art. The visit of Logan and his companion to Thomas' home village of Laugharne becomes a ritual reinactment of Thomas' life and downfall. As with "On the Death of Keats," the method of the poem is empathic, and Logan's purpose is both homage and self-confrontation.

In the poem, the ritual of pilgrimage is invariably linked with the ritual of drinking. Section one of the poem begins with a description of Caitlin Thomas' binge in Laugharne on the day of Dylan's funeral, and continues with an account of the inebriated funeral procession:

> The old pub at Brown's stays open
> long as the patrons want, for Laugharne is a little town.
> The people—even the bar-keep—stay awake and drink
> and talk of you (now famous in this place), and they tell
> the tale of Caitlin on the way to the funeral:
> she was late because she came across the street and cried
> and drank the warm pints of bitter just as you had done.
> The funeral procession weaved,
> lurched up the street toward the church.

In this passage, as in subsequent passages in the poem, the descriptions of drinking begin in a colorful fashion, but soon comes to portray a joyless and self-indulgent ritual. Section two of the poem is related with a similar ambivalence. During his journey through Wales to Laugharne, Logan does not see Thomas' legacy in the landscape that produced his poems, only reminders of Thomas' death:

> In October, month of your birth,
> my friend and I took the night train
> from London's Paddington Station past the sleep-tossed towns
> and the sheep nudging gently on the hills,
> through Swansea town where you were born
> and came to Laugharne—where you wrote your last and best
> poems—
> to follow your funeral steps.
> But first we looked where you had lived—
> saw the Laugharne castle ("brown as owls"),
> your herons standing on one leg tentative as life
> in the rich, reaching waters of the estuary,
> black as funeral priests against
> the sun, black as the crow-capped St. John's Hill where we walked
> with you up the thigh of childhood
> toward the crown and vision of age you never reached . . .

This unsettling method of description continues throughout the section. After peering into the window of the cottage where Thomas wrote his poems, Logan remarks that it "seems precarious on the ledge / above the sea," no more stable than the houseboat below it where Thomas lived with his wife and children. The final lines of the section are plaintive and somber:

> But these places are more durable than our life. They
> are more durable than our life.

In the poem's final section, as in the Keats poem, the visit to the graveside must be preceded by a descent (of sorts) into the underworld. In this case the descent begins in the form of a marathon pub-crawl, which includes each of Laugharne's seven pubs, and continues with a visit to the cemetery of Trinity churchyard, where Thomas lies buried. But while the Keats poem ends in a highly dramatic stasis, in an eerie but unresolved confrontation with death, here Logan seeks a more definite conclusion. The struggle between Eros and Thanatos that has driven the first two sections of the poem is finally resolved in—to paraphrase Thomas—a refusal to mourn. This stance should not be seen as a maudlin victory for Eros, however. What Logan seeks in the poem is perspective, an acceptance of the conflict between life force and death-instinct that dispels the gravity of their struggle. While the poem's final lines are prompted by a singularly clumsy device—Logan imagines the shade of Thomas rising out of his grave—the ending is subdued and quietly affecting:

> Dylan, you are buried up to the waist
> in the yellow leaves of autumn!
> Should I say, perhaps buried *only* up to the waist,
> for despite the melancholy in your eyes, your art,
> which you worked beneath "singing light,"
> will leave you more unburied yet?
> No. That is a trick of the heart.
> Beneath my living feet, I know
> your heavy body rots,
> and I shake like these dying aster stems among the tombs.
> Why, even the gravestones tremble
> at the touch of time. So I will touch my friend once more
> for the solace of the living—
> and for the solaces of art,
> whose mysteries deepen in the grave,
> I will read your poems again.

Logan here accomplishes what a memorable elegy ought to achieve—a triumph of the life force that is convincing, sacramental, and enduring.

There are many reservations one can voice about Logan's work, but Logan has a marvelous ability to overcome his shortcomings through a nervy generosity of spirit that none of his contemporaries can match, or would dare to match, and this generosity is strongly in evidence in his poems on literary figures. If, as Seferis writes, "a poet has only one theme—his living body," then Logan has the uncanny ability to contain within his body the physicality and aspirations of the writers who are the subjects of his poems. In recreating them through homage and elegy, he struggles to create himself, and to do so with courage and humility. Logan says as much in the discussion of elegies that concludes his essay on Thomas:

> Elegies give us again what we don't have and want. We know they are not for the dead. They are consolations for the living. Poems are resurrecting acts, recreating, saving, and perhaps damning the members of the poet's own mystical family, the parts and people he finds in himself . . . .

John Logan and family, Berkeley, California, 1982.

Biographical Note

John Logan was born in Red Oak, Iowa, in 1923. He received his B.A. in zoology from Coe College and his M.A. in English from the University of Iowa, and has done graduate work in philosophy at Georgetown University and Notre Dame. He has taught at St. John's College, the University of Notre Dame, St. Mary's College, the University of Washington, San Francisco State College, and the University of Hawaii. Since 1966 he has been Professor of English at the State University of New York at Buffalo. He is the founding editor of *Choice* and has been poetry editor for *The Nation* and *Critic*. He has been the recipient of the Morton Dauwen Zabel Award from the National Institute of Arts and Letters, and has received fellowships from the National Endowment for the Arts, the Rockefeller Foundation and the Guggenheim Foundation. *Only the Dreamer Can Change the Dream: Selected Poems* and *The Bridge of Change: Poems 1978-1980* were jointly awarded the Lenore Marshall Poetry Prize.

Bibliography

TAMA BALDWIN

Primary Works

I. POETRY

A. Books

> *Cycle for Mother Cabrini.* New York: Grove Press, 1955; Berkeley: Cloud Marauder Press, 1971; Ann Arbor: University Microfilms, 1972, 1981.
>
> *Ghosts of The Heart: New Poems.* Chicago: University of Chicago Press, 1960; New York: Phoenix Books, 1967.
>
> *Spring of The Thief: Poems 1960-1962.* New York: Alfred A. Knopf, 1963, 1967.
>
> *The Zigzag Walk: Poems 1963-1968.* New York: E.P. Dutton & Co., 1969.
>
> *The Anonymous Lover: New Poems.* New York: Liveright, 1973.
>
> *The Bridge of Change: Poems 1974-1980.* Brockport, New York: BOA Editions, 1981.
>
> *Only The Dreamer Can Change The Dream: Selected Poems.* New York: Ecco Press, 1981.
>
> *Manhattan Movements.* (In progress.)

B. Pamphlets

> *Aaron Siskind: Photographs / John Logan: Poems.* Rochester, New York: Visual Studies Workshop, 1976.
>
> *The Bridge of Change.* (Issued in December 1978 as a seasonal greeting to the friends of John Logan and of BOA Editions.) Brockport, New York: BOA Editions, 1978.
>
> *The Bridge of Change.* (Trade edition.) Brockport, New York: BOA Editions, 1978.
>
> *Only The Dreamer Can Change The Dream.* Honolulu: Petronium Press, 1975.
>
> *Poem in Progress.* Drawings: Gary H. Brown. San Francisco: Dryad Press, 1975.
>
> *Song On The Dread of a Chill Spring.* Brockport, New York: The Writers Forum, 1970.

The Transformation: Poems January–March 1981. San Francisco: Pancake Press, 1983.

C. Broadsides

"Abstract Love Poem." Buffalo, New York: Slow Loris Press, 1971.

"Cape Elizabeth, a Photograph." Cambridge, Massachusetts: Pomegranate Press, 1974.

"On Reading Camus." Buffalo: Lockwood Memorial Library, State University of New York, 1968.

"Poem for a Very Young Drinking Buddy in Albuquerque." Illustrated by K. Klopp. Cambridge, Massachusetts: Pomegranate Press, 1975.

"Poem in Progress: Part One." New York: Slow Loris Press, 1973.

D. Uncollected Poems

"The Assessment." *The Georgia Review*, 36, No. 3 (Fall 1982), 528.

"Avocado." *The Seattle Review*, IV, No. 2 (Fall 1981), 38.

"Cambridge Reverie." *Hawaii Review*, 12 (Fall 1981).

"The Feast of Friends." *New Letters*, 49, No. 2 (Winter 1982-1983), 92.

"Gallery Walk." *The Greenfield Review*, 11, No. 1-2 (Summer-Fall 1983), 1.

"Happening on Aegina." *American Poetry Review*, 11, No. 5 (September-October 1982), 48.

"Impressions of Ydra." *American Poetry Review*, 11, No. 5 (September-October 1982), 48.

"Manhattan Movements." *Memphis State Review*, 4, No. 2 (Spring 1984), 5.

"A Month of Saints." *The Kenyon Review*, NS 5, No. 1 (Winter 1983), 106.

"The Piano Scholar." *Massachusetts Review*, 23 (Summer 1982), 349.

"The Present." *Ironwood*, 9, No. 1 (Spring 1981), 80.

"Staying Awake." *Brockport Review*, No. 2, (1982), 1.

"The Transformation." *New Republic*, 18 November 1981, p. 34.

"A Verse Testament for Isabella Gardner." *Poetry Society of America Bulletin*, 72 (Winter 1982), 24-5.

"A Visit to Bill Merwin at His Hawaiian Home." *Antaeus*, No. 47 (Autumn 1982), 41.

"The Yellow Christ." *New Letters*, 49, No. 2 (Winter 1982-1983), 91.

Berg, Stephen and Robert Mezey. *The New Naked Poetry: Recent American Poetry in Open Forms.* Indianapolis: The Bobbs-Merrill Company, Inc., 1976.

Britton, Burt. *Self-Portrait: Book People Picture Themselves.* New York: Random House, 1976.

Clemente, Vince. *West Hills Review*, 1, No. 1 (Fall 1979).

Cole, William. *A Book of Love Poems.* New York: Viking, 1965.

_____. *Poetry Brief: An Anthology of Short, Short Poems.* New York: Macmillan Publishing Company, 1971.

Crang, Alan. *Tunes on a Tin Whistle: Some Real-Life Poetry.* Oxford, New York: Pergamon, 1967.

Dunning, Stephen, Edward Lueders and Hugh Smith. *Some Haystacks Don't Even Have Any Needle, And Other Complete Modern Poems.* Glenview, Illinois: Scott, Foresman and Company, 1969.

Firmage, George J. and Oscar Williams. *A Garland for Dylan Thomas.* New York: Clarke & Way, 1963.

Friebert, Stuart and David Young. *The Longman Anthology of Contemporary American Poetry 1950-1980.* New York: Longman, 1983.

Garrigue, Jean. *Translations by American Poets.* Athens: Ohio University Press, 1970.

Gildner, Gary and Judith Gildner. *Out of This World: Poems From The Hawkeye State.* Ames: The Iowa State University Press, 1975.

Hall, Donald. *Claims for Poetry.* Ann Arbor: University of Michigan Press, 1982.

_____. *Contemporary American Poetry.* Baltimore: Penguin Books, 1962, 1971, 1972.

_____. *New Poets of England and America: Second Selection.* Cleveland: The World Publishing Company, 1962.

Harris, Marguerite. *Emily Dickinson; Letters From The World.* New York: Cymric Press, 1970.

Heyen, William. *American Poets in 1976.* Indianapolis: Bobbs-Merrill Company, Inc., 1976.

Howard, Richard. *Preferences: 51 American Poets Choose Poems from Their Own Work and from The Past.* New York: Viking, 1974.

Kessler, Jascha. *American Poems: A Contemporary Collection.* Carbondale: Southern Illinois University Press, 1964.

Kostelanetz, Richard. *Possibilities of Poetry: An Anthology of American Contemporaries.* New York: Dell Publishing Company, 1970.

Ossman, David. *The Sullen Art: Interviews by David Ossman with Modern American Poets*. New York: Corinth Books, 1963.

Perlman, Jim. *Brother Songs: A Male Anthology of Poetry*. Minneapolis: HOLY Cow! Press, 1979.

Poulin, A., Jr. *Contemporary American Poetry*. Boston: Houghton Mifflin, 1971, 1975, 1980, 1985.

Rosenthal, M.L. *100 Postwar Poems, British and American*. New York: Macmillan Publishing Company, 1968.

Strand, Mark. *The Contemporary American Poets*. New York and Cleveland: The World Publishing Company, 1969.

Stryk, Lucien. *Heartland: Poets of The Midwest*. Dekalb: Northern Illinois University Press, 1967.

Williams, Miller. *Contemporary Poets in America*. New York: Random House, 1973.

II. FICTION

A. Books

The House That Jack Built; or a Portrait of The Artist as a Sad Sensualist. Illustrated by James Brunot. Omaha: Abattoir Editions, 1974; Pittsburgh: Slow Loris Press, announced for Fall, 1984.

Tom Savage; A Boy of Early Virginia. (Juvenile.) Text adapted by John Logan. Illustrated by Dan Siculan. Chicago: Encyclopaedia Britannica Press, 1962.

B. Uncollected Stories

"The Bishop's Suite." *The New Yorker*, 33, 1 June 1957, pp. 81-4. Reprinted in *Today and Tradition*. Edited by Riley Hughes. New York: Harper, 1960.

"The Cigars." *Minnesota Review*, 5, No. 1 (January-April 1965), 35-8.

"Fire!" *Big Table*, 1, No. 2 (Summer 1959), 24-7.

"House That Jack Builds." *Chicago Review*, 12, No. 3 (Autumn 1958), 26-30.

"The Last Class." *Kenyon Review*, 20 (Summer 1958), 373-92.

"The Loss." *The Critic*, 20, No. 3 (December 1961-January 1962), 26-30.

"The Panic Round." *Epoch*, XI, No. 1 (Winter 1961), 34-43. Reprinted in *Stories from Epoch*. Edited by Baxter Hathaway. Ithaca: Cornell University Press, 1966.

"The Picture for The Publisher." *New World Writing*, 11, (1957).

"The Relic." *Country Club Woman*, 1, No. 1 (1962).

"The Success." *New Letters*, 38, No. 5 (Spring 1972), 91-102. Reprinted in *The Poet's Story*. Edited by Howard Moss. New York: Macmillan Publishing Company, 1973.

III. CRITICISM: ESSAYS, REVIEWS, INTERVIEWS

A. *Collected*

A Ballet for The Ear: Interviews, Essays, and Reviews. Edited by A. Poulin, Jr. Ann Arbor: University of Michigan Press, 1983.

B. *Uncollected*

"New Catholic Poets." *The Critic*, 14, No. 2 (October-November 1960), 77-87.

"Poetry Shelf." (A regular review-column.) *The Critic*, (1962-1964).

"Priest and Poet: A Note on the Art of Raymond Roseliep." *Mutiny*, 14, No. 3 (Spring 1961), 125-9.

"The Prose of James Wright." *Ironwood*, 5, No. 2 (1977), 154-5.

"The Rilkean Sense." Review of *The Woman at The Washington Zoo*, by Randall Jarrell. *Saturday Review*, 28, (January 1961), 29-30. Reprinted in *Critical Essays of Randall Jarrell*. Edited by Suzanne Ferguson. Boston: G.K. Hall and Company, 1983.

"Six of One and Six Hundred of The Other." Review of *i; Six Non Lectures* and *Poems 1923-1954* by E.E. Cummings. *Poetry*, 86, No. 6 (September 1955), 353-8.

IV. RECORDINGS

A. *Audiotapes*

Black Box 16. Washington, D.C.: Watershed Foundation, 1979.

John Logan, Reading. Recorded 8 October 1963. San Francisco State University, American Poetry Archive.

John Logan, Reading. Recorded 27 June 1965. San Francisco State University, American Poetry Archive.

John Logan, Reading. Recorded 13 April 1966. San Francisco State University, American Poetry Archive.

John Logan, Reading. Recorded 16 May 1966. San Francisco State University, American Poetry Archive.

John Logan, Reading. Recorded 7 January 1971. San Francisco State University, American Poetry Archive.

John Logan, Reading. Recorded 17 February 1972. San Francisco State University, American Poetry Archive.

John Logan, Reading. Recorded 16 April 1980. San Francisco State University, American Poetry Archive.

Moor Swan; Suzanne. San Francisco: Dryad, 1975.

Only the Dreamer Can Change The Dream. Washington, D.C.: Watershed Intermedia, 1978.

Only The Dreamer Can Change The Dream. New York: J. Norton Sound Cassette; The Watershed Tapes of Contemporary Poetry, 1978.

Today's Poets: Their Poems, Their Voices. New York: Scholastic Records, Vol. 5, 1968.

B. *Videotapes*

The Poetry of John Logan. (Interview/Reading.) Recorded 21 April 1970. State University of New York, College at Brockport. Department of English, The Brockport Writers Forum.

The Poetry of John Logan. (Interview/Reading.) Recorded 15 February 1972. State University of New York, College at Brockport. Department of English, The Brockport Writers Forum.

The Poetry of John Logan. (Reading.) Recorded 27 April 1979. Salisbury State College, Salisbury, Maryland. Department of English, The Writers-on-the-Shore Series.

Secondary Works

I. ARTICLES

Altieri, Charles. "Poetry as Resurrection: John Logan's Structures of Metaphysical Solace." *Modern Poetry Studies*, 3, No. 3 (1973), 193-224.

Barson, Alfred. "The 'Walking' Poems: Two Recent Examples of Logan's Mature Voice." *Modern Poetry Studies*, 9, No. 3 (1979), 191-6.

Bell, Marvin. "Homage to The Runner." *American Poetry Review*, 4-5 (September-October 1975), 33-5.

———. "Logan's Teaching." *Voyages*, 6, No. 3-4 (Spring 1971-Spring 1972), 38-9.

Bly, Robert. "American Poetry: On The Way to The Hermetic." *Books Abroad*, (Winter 1972), 17-24.

_____. "John Logan's Field of Force." *Voyages*, 6, No. 3-4 (Spring 1971-Spring 1972), 29-36.

_____. "The Work of John Logan." *The Sixties*, No. 5 (1961), 77-87.

Boyers, Robert. In *Contemporary Poets*. Edited by James Vinson. New York: St. Martin's Press, 1980.

Cambon, Glauco. *Recent American Poetry*. Minneapolis: University of Minnesota Press, 1962.

Carroll, Paul. "John Logan: Was Frau Heine a Monster? or 'Yung and Easily Freudened' in Dusseldorf and Hamburg and Berlin and Paris and New York City." *Minnesota Review*, 8 (1968), 67-84. Reprinted in *The Poem in Its Skin*, by Paul Carroll. Chicago: Follett, 1968.

Chaplin, William H. "Identity and Spirit in The Recent Poetry of John Logan." *American Poetry Review*, No. 2-3 (1973), 19-24.

Cook, B. "Poet as Family Man." *St. Jude*, 28 (March 1963), 22-5.

Coulson, Joseph. "John Logan." In *Critical Survey of Poetry*. Edited by Frank N. Magill. Englewood Cliffs, New Jersey: Salem Press, 1982.

Cubbage, Elinor. "John Logan's *The Zigzag Walk*: An Anonymous Quest." *Modern Poetry Studies*, 9, No. 3 (1979), 168-78.

Dickey, James. "A Note on The Poetry of John Logan." *Sewanee Review*, 70 (1962), 257-60. Reprinted in *Babel to Byzantium*, by James Dickey. New York: Farrar, Straus & Girous, 1968.

Frumkin, Gene. "The Spiraling Notebook of John Logan." *Ironwood*, 6, No. 1 (1978), 75-86.

Howard, Richard. "The Poetry of John Logan." In *Alone in America,* by Richard Howard. New York: Atheneum, 1969.

Isbell, Harold. "Growth and Change." *Modern Poetry Studies*, 2, No. 5 (1971), 213-22.

Mazzaro, Jerome. "Ventures into Evening: Self-Parody in The Poetry of John Logan." *Salmagundi*, 2, No. 4 (1968), 78-95.

Phillips, Robert. "Quest for The Unattainable: John Logan's Anonymous Lovers." *Modern Poetry Studies*, 9, No. 3 (1979), 178-86.

Rust, Michael. "Singing for The Shadow." *Voyages*, 6, 3-4 (Spring 1971-Spring 1972), 40-7.

Thompson, Phyllis Hoge. "Journey to The New Waters of Brother, Sister." *Modern Poetry Studies*, 9, No. 3 (1979), 197-210.

II. REVIEWS

A. Cycle For Mother Cabrini

Fandel, John. *Commonweal*, 4 November 1955, p. 124.

Fitts, Dudley. *Saturday Review*, 18 February 1956, p. 50.

Fowlie, Wallace. *New York Times*, 18 December 1955, p. 4.

Joost, Nicholas. *Renascence*, 9, No. 4 (Summer 1957), 198-200.
Kunitz, Stanley. *Chicago Review*, 10, No. 2 (Summer 1956), 84.
___. *Poetry*, 88 (June 1956), 183.
US Quarterly Book Review, 12 March 1956, p. 45.

B. *Ghosts of The Heart*

Esty, Jane, and Paul Lett. *Mutiny*, 3 (Spring 1961), 163.
Frumkin, Gene. *Coast*, No. 16 (Autumn 1960), 52-3.
Hazo, Samuel. *Commonweal*, 3 February 1961, p. 489.
Houghton, Firman. *Saturday Review*, 27 August 1960, p. 22.
Rowland, S.V. *Christian Century*, 12 July 1961, p. 854.
Shapiro, Harvey. *New York Times Book Review*, 23 October 1960, p. 32.
Schmitz, Dennis. *Poetry Dialogue*, 1, No. 1 (Winter 1961), 53-5.
Smith, Ray. *Library Journal*, 15 May 1960, p. 1918.
Times Literary Supplement, 30 December 1960, p. 846.

C. *Spring of The Thief*

Bennett, Joseph. *Hudson Review*, 16, No. 4 (Winter 1963-1964), 624-33.
Fiscalini, Jane. *Commonweal*, 4 October 1963, p. 52.
Glauber, R.H. *Prairie Schooner*, 38, (Fall 1964), 279-81.
Isbell, Harold. *The Catholic Worker*, 30, No. 9 (April 1964), p. 5.
Hathaway, Baxter. *Epoch*, 13, No. 3 (Spring 1964), 275-9.
Langland, Joseph. *Sewanee Review*, 72, No. 3 (Summer 1964), 501-11.
Scott, W.T. *Saturday Review*, 26 October 1963, p. 37.
Stepanchev, Stephen. *New York Herald Tribune Books*, 11 August 1963, p. 7.

D. *The Zigzag Walk*

Booklist, 1 March 1970, p. 818.
Callahan, Patrick. *Sewanee Review*, 80, No. 4 (1972), p. 639.
Choice, 7 July 1970, p. 865.
Dickey, William. *Hudson Review*, 23, (Summer 1970), 349.
Isbell, Harold. *Commonweal*, 27 March 1970, p. 69.
Kirkus Reviews, 15 August 1969, p. 910.
Mazzaro, Jerome L. *Kenyon Review*, 32, No. 1 (1970), 163-8.
Marvin, P.H. *Library Journal*, 15 October 1969, p. 3652.
National Observer, 30 March 1970, p. 19.
Partisan Review, 38 (Winter 1971-1972), 469.
Poulin, A., Jr. *The Nation*, 29 December 1969, p. 734.
Virginia Quarterly Review, 46 (Summer 1970), 95.

E. *The Anonymous Lover*

Carpenter, John R. *Poetry*, 124 (December 1974), 166.

Cavitch, David. *New York Times Book Review*, 9 December 1973, p. 44.

Hahn, Claire. *Commonweal*, 11 January 1974, p. 371.

Hewitt, Geof. *New Letters*, 41, No. 4 (June 1975), 121-9.

Kirkus Reviews, 15 April 1973, p. 439.

Kramer, Aaron. *Library Journal*, 1 June 1973, p. 1824.

Madigan, Michael. *Michigan Quarterly Review*, 14, No. 2 (Spring 1975), 220-8.

National Observer, 18 August 1973, p. 44.

Ramsey, Paul. *Sewanee Review*, 82 (Spring 1974), 397.

Thompson, John. *Parnassus*, 2, No. 2 (Spring-Summer 1974), 66-72.

Times Literary Supplement, 29 March 1974, p. 340.

F. *Poem in Progress*

Library Journal, 1 February 1976, p. 533.

Small Press Review, 8 (November 1976), 5.

G. *The Bridge of Change*

Abbot, Steve. *Contact II,* No. 30-31 (1984), 1-3.

Coulson, Joseph. *Greenfield Review*, (Summer-Fall 1983), 6-12.

Flint, R.W. *Parnassus*, 9 (Fall 1981), 45-53.

Harmon, William. *Sewanee Review*, 41 (Summer 1983), 469-70.

Library Journal, 15 May 1981, p. 1082.

Linenthal, Mark. *San Francisco Review of Books*, 19 May 1983, p. 27.

Makuck, Peter. *Tar River Poetry*, 21, No. 2 (Spring 1982), 46-53.

Mazzaro, Jerome. *The Georgia Review*, 35 (Winter 1981), 892-6.

Murray, G.E. *Chicago Sun-Times*, 14 June 1981.

Peters, Robert. *Contact II*, No. 30-31, (1984), 1-3.

St. John, David. *Antioch Review*, 40, (Spring 1982), 225.

Sandy, Stephen. *Poetry*, 40, (August 1982), 293-305.

Smith, William J. *The Nation*, 16 October 1982, pp. 371-3.

Soldofsky, Alan. *Poetry Flash*, No. 101 (August 1981), 1-3.

Villano, Lou. *Buffalo Courier-Express*, 14 June 1981.

Williamson, Allan. *New York Times Book Review*, 21 June 1981, p. 15.

H. *Only The Dreamer Can Change The Dream*

Best Sellers, 42, July 1982, p. 156.

Booklist, 15 May 1981, p. 1082.
Book World, 2 August 1981, p. 6.
Flint, R.W. *Parnassus*, 9 (Fall 1981), 45-53.
Linenthal, Mark. *San Francisco Review of Books*, 19 May 1983,
     p. 27.
Mazzaro, Jerome. *The Georgia Review*, 35 (Winter 1981), 892-6.
Murray, G.E. *Chicago Sun-Times*, 14 June 1981.
Phillips, Robert. *The Ontario Review*, 16 (1982), 98-105.
Publishers Weekly, 20 March 1981, p. 49.
St. John, David. *Antioch Review*, 40 (Spring 1982), 225.
Smith, William J. *The Nation*, 16 October 1982, pp. 371-3.
Soldofsky, Alan. *Poetry Flash*, No. 101 (August 1981), 1-3.
Virginia Quarterly Review, 58 (Spring 1982), 59.
Williamson, Allan. *New York Times Book Review*, 21 June 1981,
     p. 15.
Wittlinger, Ellen. *Library Journal*, 106, 15 May 1981, p. 1082.

I. *A Ballet for The Ear*

Book World, 26 June 1983, p. 12.
Publishers Weekly, 25 February 1983, p. 85.

Notes on Contributors

TAMA BALDWIN is a Teaching Fellow at Ohio University where she is Assistant Editor of *The Ohio Review*. She holds graduate degrees from SUNY-Brockport and Johns Hopkins. Her poems have appeared in *Poetry*, *The Georgia Review*, and other journals.

MARVIN BELL teaches at the University of Iowa. His recent books include *Drawn by Stones, by Earth, by Things That Have Been in the Fire* (Atheneum, 1984), *Old Snow Just Melting* (University of Michigan, 1983), and (with William Stafford) *Segues: A Correspondence in Poetry* (Godine, 1983). He was a Senior Fulbright Scholar to Yugoslavia in 1983.

PETER MAKUCK teaches at East Carolina University where he edits *Tar River Poetry*. He has published a volume of poems, *Where We Live* (BOA Editions, 1982), and a collection of short stories, *Breaking and Entering* (University of Illinois, 1981).

ANTHONY PETROSKY teaches at the University of Pittsburgh. His book, *Jurgis Petraskas*, was the winner of the 1982 Walt Whitman Award of the Academy of American Poets and was published by Louisiana State University Press.

MARY RANDLETT lives on Bainbridge Island in Washington State.

DENNIS SCHMITZ lives and teaches in Sacramento. His books include *We Weep for Our Strangeness* (Big Table, 1969), *Goodwill, Inc.* (Ecco, 1976), and *String* (Ecco, 1979). A new volume, *Singing*, is forthcoming from Ecco in the spring of 1985.

LAYLE SILBERT lives in New York City. Her book, *Making a Baby in Union Park Chicago*, was published by Downtown Poets in 1983.

DAVID WOJAHN teaches at the University of Arkansas-Little Rock where he co-edits *Crazyhorse*. His book, *Icehouse Lights*, was the winner of the 1981 Yale Younger Poets Prize.

MICHAEL WATERS was born in New York City in 1949. He attended the State University of New York at Brockport, the University of Nottingham, the University of Iowa, and Ohio University. He has taught in the Creative Writing Program at Ohio University where he was Associate Editor of *The Ohio Review*, and was Visiting Professor of American Literature at the University of Athens, Greece, during 1981-82. He teaches at Salisbury State College on the Eastern Shore of Maryland. His work has appeared in numerous journals and anthologies, including *Poetry, The Yale Review, The American Poetry Review, The Georgia Review, The Missouri Review* and *The Antioch Review.* In addition to several chapbooks, he has published three full-length collections: *Fish Light* (Ithaca House, 1975) and *Not Just Any Death* (BOA Editions, 1979), and *Anniversary of the Air* (Carnegie-Mellon University Press, 1985). In 1984 he was the recipient of a Creative Writing Fellowship from the National Endowment for the Arts.

Executed in Houston, Texas, November, 1984, from original designs by Marianne Pomeroy and Steven Ford Brown. This edition is a limited first printing of 500 copies of which 450 copies have been bound in paper wrappers; 50 copies have been bound in hardcovers of which 25 copies have been signed and numbered by John Logan.